How To Reduce The Tax You Pay

How To Reduce The Tax You Pay

Completely Revised and Updated

KEY PORTER BOOKS

Canadian Cataloguing in Publication Data

Main entry under title:

How to reduce the tax you pay

Completely rev. & updated.
ISBN 1-55013-297-0 (English Canada)

ISBN 1-55013-299-7 (Quebec)

1. Tax planning – Canada – Popular works.
2. Income tax – Canada – Popular works. I. Deloitte & Touche.

HJ4661.H68 1991 343.7105'23 C90-095845-6

Key Porter Books Limited
70 The Esplanade
Toronto, Ontario
M5E 1R2

Typesetting: Computer Composition of Canada

Printed on acid-free paper

Printed and bound in Canada

90 91 92 93 94 95 6 5 4 3 2 1

The information and analysis contained in this book are not intended to substitute for competent professional advice. Planning your tax and financial affairs to reduce the tax you pay is a complex process — one that is unique to you or your business. The material that follows is provided solely as a general guide to assist you in understanding the main income tax provisions you can use to minimize your tax burden. No action should be initiated without consulting your professional advisors.

How to Reduce the Tax You Pay was compiled by a team of writers from Deloitte & Touche and (in Quebec) Samson Bélair/Deloitte & Touche, serving Canadian clients for more than 130 years. The firm is one of the largest firms of chartered accountants and management consultants, with more than 5,600 people, including 700 partners and 3,700 professional staff in some 75 Canadian centres. It serves more than 65,000 clients in Canada, including more than 100 of the *Financial Post*'s 500 top industrial companies. As a member of DRT International, the firm also serves clients in more than 100 countries around the world.

Co-Editors:

William Strain, Toronto
Gilles Veillette, Montreal

Contributors:

Gisèle Archambault, Montreal
Andy Bieber, Winnipeg
Luc Blanchette, Montreal
Marty Blatt, Edmonton
Pat Bouwers, Toronto
John Bowey, Kitchener
Nancy Braun, Toronto
Geoff Brookes, Halifax
John Budd, Markham
Jenifer Cho, Toronto
Peter Clayden, Vancouver
John Hutson, Kitchener
Bill Johnston, Ottawa
Mike Lavery, Calgary
Anne Montgomery, Toronto
Elaine Norman, Toronto
Keith Pitzel, Winnipeg
Vince Pollesel, Kitchener
Michel Richer, Montreal
Len Sakamoto, Toronto
Bill Sherman, Toronto
Terry Speiss, Winnipeg
Linda Stillabower, Toronto
Tony Tam, Toronto
Brian Taylor, Saskatoon
Bill Vienneau, Halifax
Earl Viner, Toronto

Production support:

Junia Fulgence, Toronto
Linda Gilmour, Toronto

Contents

10. Estate Planning

How To Reduce The Tax You Pay

1. The Tax Planning Process

Canadians pay many different types and amounts of taxes. Some are obvious. Others are hidden. There are retail sales taxes on consumer goods, excise taxes on items such as gasoline, alcohol, and cigarettes, and the GST. Homeowners pay property taxes. Lottery ticket purchasers pay, in effect, a tax. Most of us pay income taxes, which are usually withheld from our paycheques. Taxes influence decisions every day. They affect the amount of money we have available to consume, save, or invest.

TAX PLANNING

No one should pay more taxes than the law requires, but many Canadians do, often because they are unaware of legitimate deductions from taxable income, because they pay high marginal rates of tax on income that could be deferred to lower-rate years, or because they fall into various tax traps. Tax planning is *not* tax evasion. Tax evasion is deliberately understating income otherwise subject to tax, for example, failing to declare all your interest income on your tax return. Tax planning involves reviewing financial goals, objectives and activities, and arranging our activities to achieve our economic goals at the least tax cost. This involves using provisions of the tax law that permit us to reduce or defer taxation, increase deductions, or avoid tax traps.

"Loopholes"

Such provisions are not "loopholes". It is not loopholes in the tax law that allow some wealthy individuals to pay little or no income taxes. They do so because, through careful planning, they use incentives and other provisions in the tax law that minimize their taxable income. In contrast, loopholes are inadvertent errors in the design and structure of the law. Tax incentives are specifically implemented by law to encourage certain activities. If you take advantage of such incentives, you are doing precisely what the government encouraged you and other taxpayers to do. Unfortunately, federal finance ministers have a tendency to call tax incentives loopholes once they start becoming too popular, and to then close them down.

KEY PLANNING CONCEPTS

Tax planning essentially involves five main activities:

- income splitting – transferring income from a high tax bracket taxpayer to one in a lower tax bracket;
- income shifting – transferring income from a high tax rate year to a lower rate year; conversely, shifting deductions from a low rate year to a high rate year;
- investment selection – transforming income from a fully taxed source to one that is eligible for full or partial exemption;
- tax deferral – delaying taxation of income;

- tax shelters – using tax law incentives to maximize deductions and minimize taxable income.

Tax planning usually involves a combination of these activities and avoiding penalties (tax traps) that have been set to prevent abuses, but that may trap the unwary. Two concepts are fundamental to understanding how tax planning works. The first is the time value of money, which helps to explain tax deferral. The second is marginal tax brackets and how these change and influence our decisions.

Time Value of Money

This concept essentially says that one dollar received today is worth more to us than the same dollar received in the future. For example, if we receive one dollar today, we can put it in a savings account earning interest at, say, 10 per cent. After one year, we will have one dollar plus ten cents of interest income. If we had not received that dollar until the end of the year, we would have lost the opportunity to earn the ten cents of income.

Similarly, paying one dollar in taxes today is more expensive than doing so in the future. One dollar invested at 10 per cent will double in about seven years. If we must take that dollar out of the bank today, we will be unable to earn the interest that we could have had by leaving it in the bank.

Tax Deferral

Postponing payment of taxes is tax deferral. One major aspect of tax planning involves deferring tax payments as long as possible. The longer we are able to do so, the longer our money remains available for investment and other activities.

Marginal Tax Brackets

The second key concept in tax planning is that of marginal tax brackets. As your taxable income increases, the percentage of tax that must be paid upon that income also increases. Different tax rates at different income levels result in marginal tax brackets, which tell us how much will be paid to the government in taxes from each additional dollar of taxable income we earn.

The concept of marginal tax brackets is a key aspect of family income planning, in particular income splitting. For example, if the primary earner in the family is in a 45 per cent tax bracket and can transfer income to a family member in a 26 per cent bracket, the family will save 19 cents for every dollar of taxable income transferred (until that family member moves into the next tax bracket).

The marginal tax brackets also tell us how much we will save if we incur costs that are tax-deductible. If your marginal tax bracket is 45 per cent and you can deduct one dollar from that taxable income, it will save 45 cents in taxes; this 45-cent saving means that the actual after-tax cost of spending that tax-deductible dollar is 55 cents. Essentially, the marginal tax bracket tells us how much the government will keep of any additional dollar of income, and how much the government will pay for any additional dollar of tax-deductible expenditure.

The concept of marginal tax brackets makes tax-deductible expenditures more valuable to high-income taxpayers than to low-income taxpayers. If you are in a 45 per cent tax bracket, a $10 tax-deductible expenditure saves $4.50 in taxes. In a 26 per cent tax bracket, it saves only $2.60 in taxes.

Tax Credits versus Tax Deductions

A tax deduction decreases taxable income and saves tax based on the marginal tax bracket. A tax credit, however, is an amount subtracted to arrive at the actual tax due. It is not part of the calculation of taxable income. Thus, a tax credit of $100 will result in a tax saving of $100, regardless of the individual's marginal tax bracket.

Conversely, a $100 expenditure that results in a tax deduction will save an individual in a 45 per cent bracket $45, but will save an individual in a 26 per cent bracket only $26.

TAX PLANNING GOALS

Only you can set your planning goals, but your primary tax objective should generally be to recognize taxable income from any transaction at the time and in the form in which it will be most favourably taxed. To do so, you may want to even out yearly fluctuations in taxable income to reduce the impact of graduated tax rates, to invest in certain tax shelters, or to maximize certain deductions in high-tax years.

As you begin to set your goals, it is essential that you realize that tax planning should not be your primary objective. Your primary objective is to maximize your overall economic and financial well-being. It is unlikely that a particular tax incentive or tax plan can convert a bad investment into a good one. Suppose an investment generates tax deductions of $100, resulting in a real tax saving of about $51. If you anticipate losing the full amount you invested, your real economic cost, after the tax savings, is 49 per cent of the cost. This is not smart tax planning, nor is it a "tax shelter". This is a foolish investment!

A Word on Tax Audits

The tax authorities have three years from the time your tax return is initially assessed to review the information and make any reassessment of your taxes. Although there is an excellent chance that you never will be audited, it is important to be able to explain the information on your return if you are asked. Accordingly, one of the aspects of your financial and tax planning must be good recordkeeping. You need to document the intent and the details of your various transactions and all aspects of your business and financial activities. This documentation will assist you in remembering several years later exactly what occurred. Should the tax authorities decide to audit you, this detailed documentation also will assist you in providing evidence of careful and business-like planning, an important aspect of many areas of tax law.

There is no need to fear a tax audit. If your tax plans are well designed and well documented in accordance with tax law, there is no need for concern. Conversely, if you have made misrepresentations attributable to neglect, carelessness, or wilful default, or if you have committed fraud, you do have something to worry about! You also should note that there is no time limit for assessment on such activities!

Some tax planning possibilities cover "grey" areas of the tax law. In these cases, it is possible that upon audit there will be additional tax assessed, and it may be necessary to ask a court of law for a final determination of tax liability. If there is additional tax assessed, interest also will be assessed at prescribed rates from the time the tax originally should have been paid. Such interest is not deductible for tax purposes. For the most part, tax planning in the "grey" areas of the law is beyond the scope of this book. It is the responsibility of your professional tax consultant to advise you of any risks regarding your tax plan. It then will be your choice whether to pursue the plan with the understanding that the tax authorities may reassess your taxes. Even in "grey" areas, however, there is no need to avoid good tax planning because you fear you might be subject to an audit.

Where to Begin

Usually, the first step in effective tax planning is to find out where you stand today. Chapter 12 contains statistical tables to help you determine your tax position for 1990. This will provide a starting point for computing the tax effect of the various proposals and plans set forth in this book. Effective financial and tax planning requires:

- a realistic assessment of personal and financial goals;
- up-to-date records and financial information;
- reliable long-range projection of amount and source of income;
- as much flexibility as possible in your resources.

Outside factors may influence your choices and projections. Aspects to consider in your planning include interest rates, projected inflation rates, current income tax rules, and the possibility of future legislative changes. Once you have considered all the factors relevant to your situation and tax plan, you should be in a position to identify your choices, know when you can make them, anticipate your investment result, and decide if that is what you want.

HOW THIS BOOK CAN HELP

This book does not purport to offer or to replace professional advice, nor to review every conceivable tax planning strategy. It does highlight a number of tax planning opportunities and strategies and is intended to be a basic guide to the principles you should consider when addressing your tax planning concerns. You may wish to pursue some or all of these in more detail with your professional tax consultant.

Tax planning is essentially a simple process with a few basic elements. It should be an integral part of your regular financial planning and budgeting process, since it is a year-round activity. Unless you have planned carefully throughout the year, your opportunities for reducing your tax bill become more and more restricted as the year end approaches. Tax planning can be most effective only if begun immediately.

Get started!

2. Income and Deduction Basics

The first step as you begin to review your planning options is to look at your income. Essentially, there are three main categories of income that are taxed: employment income, business income, and income from property and capital gains. In addition, there are various other specific items of income that may or may not be taxed. As a general rule, if you have received a benefit of any kind from any activity, it is likely to be taxable. Conversely, an expenditure generally is not deductible unless it is necessary to generate a type of taxable income.

EMPLOYMENT INCOME

You probably have the least opportunity for tax planning in relation to income from employment. Your taxable employment income in most cases will include any benefit you receive by virtue of that employment. Generally, these amounts are measured by your employer and reported to you and to the government on your T4 (and Relevé 1 in Quebec) each year.

Fringe Benefits

Included in your taxable employment income are such things as personal use of the employer's auto, certain premiums paid by the employer under provincial hospitalization and medical-care plans, prizes and incentive awards, and travel benefits. On the other hand, non-taxable benefits include such things as subsidized meals, uniforms or special clothing required for the job, recreational facilities provided at your work location, discounts on merchandise you purchase from your employer for personal use, and private health and income insurance plans.

One fringe benefit that is not taxable is retirement or re-employment counselling. It is becoming more common for employers to provide such counselling to departing employees. Whether the company hires an outside consultant to provide this service to you or the company has in-house employees who provide the same service, you will not have a taxable benefit. This is also the case for counselling provided in respect of your mental or physical health and that of certain relatives.

Although there is less planning flexibility with employment income as compared to other sources of income, there are various compensation alternatives that may be available to you through your employer. A number of these have tax implications.

Employee Stock Options

If you have stock option rights as a result of employment, there are a number of factors to consider, and you should be aware of some of the ground rules if you decide to exercise the options. There are three classes of stock options to which different rules apply:

- CCPC options - offered after March 31, 1977 (April 23, 1985 in Quebec), to employees of Canadian-controlled private corporations (CCPCs);
- new options - certain qualifying options offered after February 16, 1984 (April 23, 1985, in Quebec);

- old options - all other options.

Old Rules for Options. The old rules apply to "old options" granted before February 16, 1984 (April 23, 1985, in Quebec), to non-qualifying options issued after February 15, 1984 (April 23, 1985, in Quebec), and to options granted to employees of CCPCs before April 1, 1977 (April 23, 1985, in Quebec).

The granting of a stock option does not result in an income tax liability. However, if the option is exercised or disposed of, you are deemed to have received taxable income from employment (stock option benefit) equal to the excess of the current fair market value (FMV) of the stock at the time of exercising the option over the option price. In other words, you are denied capital gains treatment, and you must bring the full amount of the increase into income at the time you exercise or dispose of the option. However, as discussed below, a deduction is allowed in arriving at taxable income if certain conditions are met.

Shares acquired under an option agreement are normally capital property with a cost base equal to their fair market value at the time of acquisition. As a result, future growth in the value of such stock would be a capital gain at the time of a future sale, while any decrease in the value would be treated as a capital loss. Such a capital gain would be eligible for the $100,000 capital gains exemption. For example, assume that:

- the option price is $4;
- the fair market value is $10 when the option is exercised;
- the subsequent sale in 1990 realizes $13.

The stock option benefit from such a transaction would be $6 ($10 - $4) and would be taxed as employment income at the time the shares are acquired for the option price of $4. When the shares are sold in 1990, there is a capital gain of $3 ($13 - $10), three-fourths of which is included in taxable income. (A pending technical amendment to the law would clarify that the benefit otherwise determined is to be reduced by any amount paid by the employee to acquire the stock option as well as any amount paid for the shares themselves.)

You should remember that you will have taxable employment income on the sale of an option to an unrelated party. If you transfer the option to a related party, you will have taxable income at the time the related party exercises the option, in the same manner as if you had exercised the option.

Post-February 15, 1984 (April 23, 1985, in Quebec) Options. If a qualifying stock option is granted after February 15, 1984 (April 23, 1985, in Quebec), you will be entitled to a tax deduction upon exercise or disposing of the option (upon disposition of the shares in Quebec) equal to one-fourth (after 1989) of the stock option benefit included in income. In the above example, you would be entitled to deduct $1.50 (one-fourth of $6) from the $6 taxable benefit in arriving at taxable income when the option is exercised (when the shares are sold in Quebec). In effect, this subjects the increase in value to the date of acquisition to tax at capital gains rates but ensures that the gain does not qualify for the capital gains exemption.

For a stock option to qualify for this treatment, the exercise price of the option must be equal to or greater than the market value of the stock at the time the option was granted. In addition, the employee must be at "arm's length" with the corporation. (This means that the employee may not be a shareholder who controls the corporation, be a member of a group that controls the corporation, or be related to any such persons.) There also are conditions that the shares must meet, which essentially ensure that they are common shares.

Employee Stock Options: Canadian-controlled Private Corporation Rules. Preferred treatment is provided to employees who are granted a stock option after March 31, 1977 (April 23, 1985, in Quebec), if the following conditions are met:

- The employer corporation is a Canadian-controlled private corporation, and the stock is issued by a Canadian-controlled private corporation that does not deal at arm's length with the employer (usually they are one and the same).

- The employee is dealing at arm's length with the corporation immediately after the exercise of the option. This would exclude a controlling shareholder and the members of his or her family.

- The employee has not disposed of the share within two years of acquiring it (except as a result of death).

If these conditions are met and the option is exercised after May 22, 1985, a taxable benefit from employment, equal to the difference between the exercise price of the shares and the fair market value of the shares when the option was exercised, will arise in the year the shares are actually sold by the employee. In the above example, a $6 taxable benefit ($10 minus $4) per share must be included in the employee's income in the year the shares are sold for $13. The full amount of this benefit is included in income. However, if the shares were owned for at least two years prior to disposition, a deduction equal to one-fourth (after 1989) of the benefit is allowed in arriving at taxable income, even if the exercise price ($4) was less than the fair market value at the time the option was granted. (If the disposition is a result of death, this deduction is allowed regardless of how long the shares were owned.) The $3 remaining portion of the gain ($13 minus $10) is a capital gain eligible for the $100,000 capital gains exemption.

If the above conditions are met, and you have stock you acquired through an option before May 23, 1985, at the time of disposition of this stock, you will have a capital gain equal to the proceeds you receive minus the option price you paid. However, the amount of gain prior and subsequent to exercise of the option is eligible for the capital gains exemption.

Since a private corporation's shares are not readily marketable, for his own protection a prospective purchaser should consider a buy/sell agreement. This is an agreement entered into between the shareholders of a corporation wherein, among other things, a shareholder who retires from employment, or who dies, is guaranteed that his shares will be purchased by the remaining shareholders or the corporation itself. The price at which the shares will be purchased is predetermined in the agreement, or will be determined by a formula set forth in the agreement.

The shares of a private corporation may be less attractive as part of an employment compensation package in the future. This is due to the decreased tax benefits available through stock options, together with the lack of marketability of the shares. You might want to consider discussing alternatives such as "phantom stock plans" with your employer.

Interest Expense. If the exercise of the option is financed by borrowed money, the interest expense incurred may be deducted from all sources of income for tax purposes. However, the expense will form part of your cumulative net investment loss (CNIL) for the purpose of calculating your capital gains exemption. (The CNIL rules are discussed in Chapter 7.)

Employee Loans

The term "employee loan" is commonly used today to describe any situation in which the employee may be taxed on any imputed interest benefit resulting from indebtedness to an employer. However, employee loan is a misnomer. The benefit rules apply not only to loans but to any other form of debt incurred by virtue of the office or employment (prospective or current) of an individual. It is not necessary that the employee be the debtor, nor is there any requirement that the employer be the creditor. For example, the imputed interest rules will apply in cases where the employer makes a loan to the employee's child to help support his or her university education, or where an employee obtains a bank loan at a below-market interest rate due to the employer's involvement. Regardless of the actual debtor, any imputed interest benefit will be taxable in the hands of the employee.

The amount of the taxable benefit to be included in income is generally calculated as the difference between interest actually paid within the year or 30 days after the end of the calendar year, and interest that would be paid using the prevailing prescribed interest rate, which is set by the Government each quarter. For example, if you borrow $10,000 from your employer at 4 per cent and the prescribed rate is 10 per cent all year, you must include $600 in income as a taxable benefit (10 per cent minus 4 per cent times $10,000), assuming the loan is outstanding for the entire year.

Home Purchase Loans. A home purchase loan is a loan that enables the borrower or a related person to acquire a dwelling to be inhabited by him or her, or to refinance a mortgage on such a dwelling. (A pending technical amendment to the law would expand the definition to include a loan used to acquire a share of a cooperative housing corporation entitling the purchaser or a related person to inhabit a dwelling unit owned by such corporation.)

The taxable benefit on home purchase loans is determined using the lesser of the prescribed rate of interest for the current period and the prescribed rate at the time the loan was made. (The prescribed rate for this purpose for 1990 was 13 per cent for the first half of the year and 14 per cent for the rest of the year.) All home purchase loans are considered to have a term not exceeding five years, so that on each fifth anniversary date of the loan, a new loan is deemed to be received, and the prescribed rate of interest at that time applies for the next five-year period.

Because of the way the prescribed rate is calculated, one knows in advance what the rate will be in the following quarter. Knowing the prescribed rate in advance provides a planning opportunity. An employee who is arranging a loan from his or her employer to acquire (or to repay a loan that had been used to acquire) a home should consider requesting a short-term loan initially (i.e., less than three months). If the prescribed rate for the next quarter is lower than (or the same as) the current quarter, another short-term loan can be arranged. If the prescribed rate for the next quarter is higher, a long-term (e.g., five-year) loan could be finalized in the current quarter.

Home Relocation Loans. When an employee relocates or takes up a new position after May 23, 1985, is eligible to claim moving expenses, and has received a low-interest or interest-free loan to assist with the acquisition of a home at the new location, he or she will be able to deduct a specified amount of the taxable benefit relating to this home purchase loan in arriving at taxable income. The deduction would equal the lesser of the actual benefit included in income and the benefit from a $25,000 interest-free employee loan. This deduction will be available for the lesser of five years or the length of time the home purchase loan (or a replacement loan for it) is outstanding. In general, moving expenses may be claimed if the employee's new residence is at least 40 kilometres closer to the new work location than his previous residence.

Commercial Rate Rule. The taxable benefit rules do not apply to an employee loan on which interest is charged at a rate equal to or above the commercial lending rate, having regard to all the terms and conditions of the loan, available at the time the loan was made. The rules do apply, however, to third-party loans where the employer is financing part or all of the cost of funds.

Deductibility of Imputed Interest. Employees may treat as deductible interest expense any imputed interest included in income as a taxable benefit, provided such interest otherwise would be deductible if it were actually paid. This will make low-interest or interest-free loans an extremely attractive perquisite of employment if the proceeds of the loan are used for investment purposes, including investment in shares of an employer corporation, or for the purchase of an automobile or aircraft used in the business of the employer. You will, of course, want to consider the tax treatment of automobiles used for business purposes, discussed in Chapter 9.

Note, however, that any potential deduction is available only to the debtor even though the interest benefit may be included in another taxpayer's (i.e., the employee's) income. Where there is a potential interest deduction, it is likely best to ensure that the employee is the debtor; otherwise the employee will have the taxable benefit but not the offsetting deduction. If, however, the debtor is in a higher tax bracket than the employee, it would be advantageous for the deduction to be in the hands of the debtor.

Benefits from Employee Loans. Interest-free or low-interest loans can produce a worthwhile benefit even if interest is imputed as a taxable benefit since the imputed rates often result in a rate less than the employee would pay in the marketplace. Assuming that you borrow $25,000 from your employer at 13 per cent and otherwise would have had to borrow at 15 per cent, you will save $500 each year in interest charges. No taxable benefit arises because the rate of interest you pay is greater than or equal to the prescribed rate (assuming that the prescribed rate does not exceed 13 per cent). Note that the interest would have to be paid by January 30 of the following year; otherwise it would not reduce the imputed benefit.

Of course, the benefits are even greater if the employee loan is interest-free. If your marginal rate of tax is 44 per cent and you borrow $25,000, your cost of the loan is the tax paid on the imputed benefit of $3,250 ($25,000 at 13 per cent), which is $1,430 (assuming the prescribed rate is 13 per cent throughout the year and the loan is outstanding for a full year). This works out to an effective interest charge of 5.72 per cent and a savings of $2,320 compared to the 15 per cent loan ($3,750 minus $1,430). If the loan is used to earn investment income, the imputed interest of $3,250 is deductible and there is no cost associated with the loan, whereas your after-tax cost on a conventional loan would be $2,100 ($3,750 less tax saving at 44 per cent).

Shareholder Loans. If you are a shareholder as well as an employee, there are special rules you must consider regarding loans or advances from your company. Although many of the rules regarding low-interest and interest-free loans are the same, there are greater tax implications regarding the granting of such loans. See Chapter 3.

Pensions, Deferred Profit Sharing Plans, Salary Deferral Arrangements, etc. There are a number of plans offered by employers to defer income for employees. Many of these take the form of retirement planning. Qualification for deferral of current taxation on employment income will depend on the nature of your particular plan. See Chapter 6.

Expenses Connected with Employment

Generally, employees are not entitled to claim deductions for expenditures they incur as a result of their employment, unless such deductions are specifically authorized in the Income Tax Act. Employment expenses that may be deductible include such items as union or professional dues (not including the initiation fee), automobile expenses, and moving expenses. Special expense deduction provisions are provided for clergymen, travelling salesmen, and certain railway and transport employees. If you qualify, be sure you have the appropriate prescribed forms signed by your employer.

Legal expenses paid after 1985 to collect or establish a right to a retiring allowance (which includes rewards for wrongful dismissal) or pension benefit are deductible. The deduction is limited to the amounts received that are not transferred to an RRSP or RPP. Excess amounts can be carried forward for deduction in any of the seven following years. Any reimbursement of these fees must be included in income.

In addition, effective January 1, 1989, an individual certified as having a severe and prolonged impairment may deduct, to a maximum of $5,000, the costs of care provided by a part-time unrelated adult attendant. The deduction is limited to two-thirds of eligible income, which includes income from employment or self-employment, a training allowance, or a grant for research or similar work (net of expenses). This deduction is in addition to the personal tax credit that may be claimed by such a certified person. See Chapter 5.

Automobile Expenses

If you use your own automobile for your employer's business, or in your own business, you may be entitled to deduct automobile expenses. See Chapter 9.

Moving Expenses

Moving expenses are deductible provided you meet certain conditions and the expenses are not reimbursed by your employer. The moving expenses must be incurred in connection with beginning a business, employment, or full-time post-secondary education at a new location. In addition, the distance between your old residence and your new work or school location must be at least 40 kilometres greater than the distance between your new residence and your new work or school location.

The expenditures that will qualify as deductible moving expenses are fairly broad. They include the travelling costs to move you, your family, and your household goods and include such things as meals and lodging en route. Also included are selling costs in respect of your old residence and legal services in respect of the purchase of the new residence. You also may deduct storage costs for your household goods incurred in the course of the move, as well as other items. There are various limits on the total amount that will be deductible, depending on the particular circumstances of your move.

BUSINESS INCOME

Income from Business or Property

If an activity is a business, you generally are taxed on the "profit" from that business, as measured by the revenue generated minus the expenses incurred in generating the revenue. If you realize a loss on the activity, this loss may offset income from employment, investment income, and so forth. (If the losses are generated from farming, their availability to offset other types of income including income from other businesses is restricted in certain circumstances.)

If the activity gives rise to income from property, the income either will be fully includible in calculating taxable income, or it will be a capital gain, eligible for a partial exclusion and the capital gain exemption.

The economic reality of the activity should control its tax treatment. However, it is absolutely critical in this area of law that you have detailed documentation of your activity. If you are starting a new business while you remain employed, you must maintain detailed records to demonstrate that you have a reasonable expectation of profit from the business, and that you are approaching the business in a professional manner. This includes obtaining business-like advice, if necessary, and demonstrating that you either have abilities in the field or are seeking guidance. If you cannot demonstrate expectation of profit and a business-like approach to the activity, you may be treated as having a hobby. If so, your tax deductions will be restricted to the income generated from the activity. If the activity generates a loss, you will not be able to offset the loss against other income. Maintaining such records is particularly important for activities such as farming, which are frequently done on a part-time basis. If your activity generates losses for a number of years, the tax authorities are strongly inclined to view it as a hobby rather than a business.

Conversely, if you have entered into the activity as an investment, hoping to use the property acquired to generate income, it is equally important that you document this intent and provide evidence that it is reasonable to expect that the property will give rise to investment income. For example, if you buy a piece of land, expecting to build an office building or some other income-generating asset, the land may be a capital asset eligible for capital gains treatment on disposition. If, on the other hand, the investment in the land was made with the intention of holding the land to generate income from its rise in value, this would be considered an adventure in the nature of trade, or a business (depending on the volume of similar activity), and would result in fully taxable income. (The tax authorities are more inclined to treat increases in value as ordinary income and decreases in value as capital than they are to treat increases as capital and decreases as ordinary income.)

Taxation of Income from a Business

Generally, there are more opportunities for tax planning if you are self-employed or own a business than there are for employees. Different tax rules apply to business income. In addition, taxation of income from your business will differ depending upon whether the business is operated in corporate or unincorporated form. (See Chapter 8 for a discussion of the advantages and disadvantages of incorporation, as well as a number of aspects of tax planning for small businesses.) Note that you may transfer assets from an unincorporated business to a partnership or a corporation on a tax-deferred basis, subject to certain restrictions.

Generally, you will be taxed on the "profit" from your business, regardless of how much you withdraw from the business (assuming your business is unincorporated). Profit is measured by calculating income from the business and subtracting various expenses that are allowed as deductions. These expenses must be reasonable in amount and must be incurred for the purpose of generating income. Common deductions include expenditures for salaries, supplies, rent, advertising, and so forth. The amounts spent for enduring items such as furniture or equipment are not deductible, but you may claim capital cost allowances (depreciation) for such acquisitions. The profit from your business will be included in your taxable income in the calendar year during which the fiscal year of your business ends.

Home Office Expenses

If you are self-employed or run your own sideline business and have an office in your home, you may be able to deduct expenses relating to that office. For home office expenses to be deductible for fiscal periods commencing after 1987, the office must be either your principal place of business, or must be used exclusively to earn business income and be used on a regular and continuous basis for meeting clients, customers or patients. The amount deducted cannot exceed the income from the business for the year, after deducting all other expenses. Any excess amount may be carried forward to be deducted in years when the business generates income. (A pending technical amendment to the law would essentially extend these rules to home office expenses of employees, starting with the 1991 taxation year.)

Taxation Year

In the first year of business operations, you must select a fiscal year for your business. If you expect increasing income from the business, you should select a fiscal year-end occurring early in the calendar year. This enables you to take advantage of some deferral on the income generated from the business in the latter part of the year, since that income does not become subject to tax until the following calendar year.

For example, assume you started your business on July 1, 1990. If you selected December 31, 1990, as the first fiscal year end of the business, you have to include the profit from July 1 to December 31 with income on your 1990 tax return. However, if you chose January 31, 1991 as the first fiscal year end, then you would not have to include any income for tax purposes until you file your 1991 return. However, if you incurred a loss for the period July 1 to December 31, 1990, you might wish to choose December 31 as the first year end, so as to use the loss incurred to offset other income earned in 1990. Similarly, if you earned a profit from July 1990 to December 31, 1990, but incurred losses in January, February and March 1991, you would probably wish to select March 31 as the fiscal year end.

Once a year end is selected, it must be retained, unless the tax authorities permit you to change it. Usually, permission will be given only if there is a valid business reason to change it. Tax planning or tax saving is not accepted as a valid business reason. Therefore, the choice of a fiscal year end should not be determined solely for short-term tax savings.

PROPERTY INCOME AND CAPITAL GAINS

The third major income category is income from property, including interest, dividends and rent. Capital gains are connected with property income, but are a separate category because of the special rules for the taxable amounts. See Chapter 7.

Gains from transfers (sales, gifts, etc.) of property generally are taxable, including gains from sales of property used solely for personal purposes. The primary exceptions to this rule are certain tax-deferred transfers between spouses, and gains from the sale of a personal residence. Transfers between spouses and others are discussed in Chapter 4.

Deductible Interest

In general, if you borrow funds and the funds are used to earn income, any interest expense incurred is deductible from income, with certain exceptions. Earning income does not necessarily mean that you have to earn a profit immediately; there only need be a reasonable expectation of profit; therefore incurring a loss does not prejudice the deductibility of the interest expense. However, the tax authorities may disallow the portion of the interest expense that exceeds the return on your investment, if it was reasonably foreseeable, at the time the loan was taken out, that the rate of interest would exceed the rate of return in the future.

Interest expense is deductible only if you own the related investment throughout the period of time the funds were borrowed. For example, if you borrow $1,000 to purchase shares, but you sell the shares after only two months, interest for the period after the date of sale is not deductible. If you sold the shares for $400 and purchased other stock immediately for this amount, a portion of the interest ($400/$1,000) would then be deductible. You could not deduct the portion of the interest related to the loss realized on the sale of the shares.

You are never allowed to deduct the interest on funds borrowed for personal expenditures, such as interest on money borrowed to finance a vacation or purchase a home. Thus, you should attempt to channel all your borrowing into income-earning investments (or better still, borrow only for business purposes) and pay for personal expenditures out of your savings. However, you are permitted to deduct interest when a personal asset (such as your home) has been used as collateral for a loan to finance an investment.

Principal Residence

You will not be taxable on the gain on disposition of a residence if you meet the principal residence exemption rules. Only the ownership interest in one home can be designated as your principal residence for a particular year. You can make the designation only for years you are resident in Canada. In addition, for years after 1981, only one principal residence per family unit per year is allowed, rather than the one unit per person per year that was allowed prior to 1982.

A house, condominium, mobile home, trailer, houseboat, or a share in a cooperative housing corporation qualifies. It can be owned outright, or jointly with one or more other individuals. In addition, it does not have to be located in Canada in order to qualify. (Tax might be payable in the other country on the disposition.)

For the home to be your principal residence, you or your spouse or a child must be ordinarily resident in the home during the designated year. Usually the family home is designated, but a part-time residence, such as a summer cottage, can qualify.

Your lifetime capital gains exemption is not affected by a tax-exempt gain on your principal residence.

Post-1981 Principal Residence Rules. Beginning in 1982, a family unit is able to designate only one home under the principal residence rules with respect to each year. In any particular year, a family unit consists of you, your spouse (provided you were married throughout the year and were not throughout the year living apart and legally separated) and children who were throughout the year unmarried and under 18 years of age. This means that if you and your spouse each own a home, you will be liable for tax on all or a portion of the capital gain accruing on one of the homes beginning January 1, 1982. This gain is eligible for the $100,000 capital gains exemption. When a couple marries after 1981 and each owns a home, each may designate his or her home for the year of marriage and prior years, but only one home may be designated after the year of marriage.

Determining the Taxable Portion. Subtract the exempt portion from the total gain on the sale. The remainder, if any, is subject to normal capital gains rules (three-fourths includible in income after 1989, but also eligible for the lifetime capital gains exemption).

The exempt portion is based on the number of years that the property was a principal residence compared to the number of years of ownership. The actual rules are complicated. However, if you can designate the property as your principal residence for all years of ownership, or all years except one, the total gain is generally exempt.

Special transitional rules apply where a property owned on December 31, 1981, is subsequently sold. The rules provide that the non-exempt portion of the gain is the lesser of two amounts. Both amounts are calculated on the same basis as outlined above. One calculation is done by viewing the total years of ownership as one period (i.e., the normal method) and the other calculation is done by separating the years of ownership into two periods, one pre-1982 and one post-1981. In order to do this latter calculation, the fair market value of the property on December 31, 1981, must be determined.

Although these rules were designed to provide transitional relief to families with more than one home, they also apply to single-home families. These rules may be beneficial where a portion of the gain is taxable because your principal residence designation is not available for all the years of ownership (e.g., you were not a Canadian resident for several years) and either the home declined in value after December 31, 1981, or the bulk of the gain is attributed to the period before 1982.

Designating a Property as a Principal Residence. If, during the year, you dispose of a property that you wish to claim as your principal residence and a portion of the gain is subject to tax, you must file a prescribed form with your tax return for that year designating it as your principal residence for the years chosen. If the gain is completely exempt from tax, the tax authorities do not require the form to be filed.

If you have more than one family home and must decide which home to designate and for how many years, the decision can be quite complex. Consider consulting your professional advisor prior to the sale.

Planning. If your family currently has, or intends to acquire, a second home, record all capital costs associated with your homes. These would include the costs of adding a pool, finishing the basement, or adding an extra room. Unless a record is kept of such expenditures, you may have to compute any ultimate gain using the original purchase price as the cost base of the property, which may be much lower than the total invested in the property. In addition, if the family has only one house, consider transferring the ownership of the personal residence to the lower-income spouse. See Chapter 4.

To Sell or Not to Sell. Consider retaining your residence if you are leaving on an indefinite or temporary basis. During your absence, you may rent your home and still retain your ability to designate it as your principal residence for the years in which you were living there and, provided certain conditions are met, for up to four years after that. In addition, during the years of rental, you may deduct various costs and expenses. If you currently live in a high-cost area for housing, retaining the home will protect you from significant price increases while you are away. If you sell the residence instead of re-occupying it, the gain that accrued during years in which you designate the home as a principal residence will be tax-free. The gain that accrued during years when the residence was rented may not be taxable if you were away less than five years. Even if all or part of this gain is taxable, you still will benefit from the increased appreciation.

Special rules will extend the four-year maximum period referred to above if the housing unit is not occupied as a result of your employer or your spouse's employer requiring that you or your spouse relocate. Certain conditions must be met to take advantage of this extension.

Other special rules apply if a housing unit was originally acquired as a principal residence and was later used to earn rental or business income on a permanent basis. They also apply where the unit was originally acquired to earn rental or business income and was later used as a principal residence on a permanent basis. The rules defer the recognition of the resulting capital gain until disposition of the housing unit.

Rental Expenses

If you own investment property and earn rental income, you may deduct all the current expenses you incur with respect to the rental property and claim capital cost allowance (CCA) on the property itself. However, CCA cannot be used to create or increase a loss with respect to a rental property. It can offset only the net rental income on the property prior to the CCA claim.

Current expenses include the cost of advertising for tenants, heat, hydro, property taxes, water rates, insurance, and labour and material for routine repairs and maintenance. Capital expenditures such as major additions or renovations are not deductible but can usually be added to the capital cost of the property and then be claimed more slowly as CCA.

If you rent out part of your principal residence, the same basic rules apply for current expenses. Expenses fully attributable to the rented portion are fully deductible. Common expenses such as heat, hydro, and property taxes must be prorated so that only the portion that relates to the rented part of the principal residence is deducted from rental income. You may claim CCA for the rented portion, but you may not want to take this deduction because doing so will erode part of your principal residence exemption and cause a portion of any gain on a subsequent sale to be taxable.

OTHER INCOME

Income from sources other than employment, business, or property is probably taxable, although certain receipts, such as lottery winnings, may be tax-free. If you have doubts about the taxation of a particular item, you should seek professional advice.

Alimony and Maintenance Payments

If you are divorced or separated, you may be receiving (or paying) amounts of alimony and/or maintenance. Generally, such payments are includible in your income in the year of receipt (and deductible for the payer in the same year). If the payment is taxable income to one party, it is an allowable deduction to the other. If the income is not taxable, the payment is not deductible.

Alimony or maintenance must be:

- periodic;
- pursuant to a decree, judgment, or written agreement;
- made for the maintenance of the recipient and/or children.

In addition, the parties to the agreement must be living apart pursuant to a divorce, judicial separation, or written separation agreement, from the time of the payment until the end of the year. There are any number of complexities with respect to alimony and maintenance payments. These include whether the payments are periodic alimony or maintenance versus instalments of lump-sum obligations. Another question is the qualification of payments made to third parties as alimony or maintenance, for example, payments made to the holder of the home mortgage. You should note that voluntary additional payments that are not part of the agreement will not qualify. It is prudent to have competent legal and tax advice regarding separation and/or divorce agreements.

Frequently alimony and maintenance agreements result in income shifting from a higher-income individual to a lower-income individual. As a result, there are tax benefits inherent in the payments because the higher-income individual obtains a deduction that saves a greater amount of tax than the corresponding tax cost to the recipient of the payment. Because of the shifting aspects of these payments, many separation or divorce agreements are negotiated on an after-tax basis.

Annuities

An annuity is an agreement for periodic payments over a specified period of time. It may be purchased with after-tax or before-tax dollars. For example, investing RRSP funds in an annuity contract uses before-tax dollars, while buying an annuity contract from savings uses after-tax dollars.

If an annuity payment is received from a contract purchased through a tax-exempt fund or plan, the full amount of the payment is includible in your taxable income in the year of receipt. Most common examples of such annuity payments include amounts from pension plans, RRSPs, and so forth.

If you have purchased the annuity with personal funds rather than through a tax-exempt plan, a portion of each payment under the contract is excludible from your taxable income. This portion represents your original investment in the contract, which already has been taxed.

Gifts and Inheritances

The recipient of a gift or inheritance does not have taxable income. The transferor is considered, with certain exceptions such as spousal transfers, to have sold the property at its fair market value at the date of transfer. Thus, the transferor will have taxable income on any accrued gains, while the recipient will be treated as having acquired the property at the fair market value at date of transfer.

Lotteries, Gambling, and Other Prize Winnings

Gains resulting from activities where the primary factor in determining whether there will be a gain is chance (e.g., lotteries and gambling) are not included in income. However, prizes related to your employment are likely to be considered as connected with services rendered and thus taxable as employment income.

Other Deductions

Generally, personal expenditures are not deductible for tax purposes. However, you may deduct such miscellaneous items as investment counselling and portfolio management fees, safekeeping fees, and fees for a self-administered RRSP.

Child Care Expenses

This deduction is a maximum of $2,000 per child under age 14 at any time during the year, with no family maximum (previously there was an $8,000 cap). The maximum per child is increased to $4,000 for claims in respect of severely disabled children and children under seven years of age at the end of the year. Although there is no maximum dollar limit, the deduction is restricted to two-thirds of earned income and must be claimed by the lower-income spouse.

3. Income Deferral

Income deferral simply means deferring the recognition of income for tax purposes to future years. The benefit of income deferral is that the payment of tax on that income is postponed. It is sometimes said that tax deferred is tax saved. If, for example, you can defer $1,000 of tax payable for one year and earn 10 per cent during that time, you have "saved" $100 (less, of course, any tax payable on that $100 of income).

Since 1983, there has been a significant drop in the number of opportunities to defer income, especially with respect to interest income, which must be reported annually even if it has not yet been received. These rules affect all taxpayers, including individuals and trusts with individuals as beneficiaries. However, income earned in deferred income plans, including registered retirement savings plans, deferred profit sharing plans and registered pension plans, is not affected by these changes.

Three-Year Accrual Rules

The former three-year accrual rules apply only to debt obligations acquired before 1990, but they apply to all debt obligations other than income bonds and debentures, Salary

Deferral Arrangements (SDAs), Small Business Bonds (SBBs) and Small Business Development Bonds (SBDBs). Revenue from debt obligations acquired by an individual before November 13, 1981, does not have to be treated as income before receipt of the revenue, provided the following conditions are met:

- the maturity date was not extended;
- the terms or conditions relating to the repayment of the principal amount were not changed; and
- the holder could not require the repayment, acquisition, cancellation or conversion of the obligation, other than by reason of a failure or default under the terms or conditions of the obligation.

If an obligation held by an individual is subject to the three-year accrual rules, on every third anniversary date of the obligation, the individual must include in income any interest accrued after December 31, 1981, that was not previously included in income.

The "third anniversary" date is three years after December 31 of the calendar year in which the obligation was issued, and every third year thereafter. For purposes of determining the third anniversary date, obligations acquired before 1982 are deemed to have been issued on December 31, 1988; accordingly, an income inclusion would not be required until the first "third anniversary" date, namely, 1991.

You may elect in your tax return to include in income interest accrued to the end of the year on a debt obligation that was not previously included in income. Once made, the election applies to that particular debt obligation for each subsequent year in which the taxpayer holds the obligation. Don't forget to think ahead. If you still hold investments that are subject to the three-year accrual rule and the operation of these rules will push your income into a higher tax bracket, you might be better off reporting the income annually. This is likely beneficial only if you would otherwise move from being taxed at the 17 per cent federal rate to the 26 per cent or 29 per cent federal rate. In making this election, however, remember that you must balance the tax saving against the fact that in future years you will also end up prepaying tax.

The interest accrual rules also apply where an individual holds an investment interest in a life insurance policy, including an annuity contract. The rules do not apply to "exempt policies", nor to most investment interests held before December 2, 1982. Certain prescribed annuity contracts are also exempt from the accrual rules.

Annual Accrual Rules

The April 1989 federal budget proposed the replacement of the three-year accrual rules with annual accrual rules for the investment instruments discussed above. These rules were enacted into law as this book went to press, and they will apply to such investments acquired after 1989; all taxpayers will be required to report accrued income on an annual basis. You should be aware that an investment is treated as having been acquired after 1989 if, after that year, the term of the investment has been extended or the investment has been materially altered.

An obligation that is subject to the annual accrual rules requires, on the first anniversary date of the instrument, an inclusion in income of any interest that has accrued after December 31, 1989 and was not previously included in income. The first anniversary date is the day that is one year after the day immediately preceding the date on which the obligation was issued and every year thereafter.

Issuers of investments subject to the proposed rules, including the Bank of Canada, will be required to provide annual information slips to the holders of the instruments showing the amount of interest accrued to each anniversary date of the investment. Those who supply information returns must now include the Social Insurance Number of the individual to whom that information return relates. This enhanced Social Insurance Number reporting will allow Revenue Canada to match information slips more easily with the appropriate individual.

In the budget of May 16, 1989, the Quebec Minister of Finance confirmed his intention to implement the same changes for Quebec tax purposes. Unlike the federal system, these measures had not been ratified at press time but they will nevertheless be applied starting in 1990.

If a taxpayer acquires a "prescribed debt obligation", interest is deemed to accrue on the obligation in a manner prescribed by regulation. Prescribed debt obligations include zero interest bonds, bonds that areheld without also holding the related bond interest coupons, and the interest coupons stripped from such bonds.

Planning Around the Accrual Rules. It goes without saying that before investing in deferred income securities or annuities, you should take maximum advantage of deferred income plans where you are not required to report income on an annual accrual basis. These include registered retirement savings plans (RRSPs) and registered pension plans (RPPs).

The earnings inside such plans are completely sheltered from tax until you withdraw funds from the plan. RRSP and RPP contributions are generally deductible from income in the current year and payments from a plan can be postponed well into your retirement. Since the deferral is for the long term, you will generally benefit no matter what your marginal tax rate is when you eventually withdraw the funds.

For example, assume that you have the option of contributing $5,000 to an RRSP from which you will begin receiving a retirement income in 20 years. Your marginal tax rate now is 40 per cent, and in the table below it is assumed that your marginal rate in 20 years is either 30 per cent or 40 per cent. To keep the example simple, it is assumed you pay tax on the RRSP amount in a lump sum in the twentieth year, which of course would probably not be the case. The RRSP earns interest at the rate of 10 per cent over the 20 years.

Marginal Tax Rate	After-tax Amount Available
30%	$23,546
40%	$20,182

If you did not make the RRSP contribution and paid tax at 40 per cent on the $5,000, you would have $3,000 left to invest. Assuming your annual after-tax return is 6 per cent (after paying tax at the rate of 40 per cent on 10 per cent earnings), you will accumulate $9,621 in 20 years, which is $10,561 less than you would accumulate by contributing to the RRSP (40 per cent tax rate after 20 years).

The advantage comes about because the before-tax amounts in the RRSP accumulate interest on a tax-free basis, while your after-tax earnings outside the plan are taxed each year and you have a smaller amount available for reinvestment. In addition, under the RRSP you are able to pay your taxes in the future with inflated dollars that are worth much less than today's dollars.

You may also want to consider the possibility of deferring tax by acquiring capital property. The accrual rules do not apply to unrealized capital gains. High yield preferred shares may prove suitable, since they offer an attractive dividend with the possibility of capital gains. And the $100,000 lifetime capital gains exemption ($500,000 for qualified farming property and shares of small business corporations) makes owning capital property even more attractive.

Tax Assistance for Retirement Saving

Perhaps the easiest way to defer income to future years is to make tax-deductible contributions to RRSPs or RPPs. These plans are affected by the new system of improved tax assistance for retirement saving, to be phased in over the next few years. For a more comprehensive analysis of the retirement saving rules related to RRSPs, see Chapter 6.

Retiring Allowances

To a certain extent, a retiring allowance can be considered as a means of deferring income. However, it must not take the form of a deferred salary, which would be the case if an employee accepted a relatively low salary in exchange for a generous "so-called" retiring allowance.

A retiring allowance is defined as an amount (other than a superannuation or pension benefit or an amount received as a consequence of the death of an employee) received by the taxpayer on or after the retirement of any person in recognition of long service, including early retirement incentives or any payment received in respect of a loss of employment, whether or not received as a termination payment or damages from loss of office. Hence, termination payments are fully taxable, although the tax may be deferred by transferring eligible amounts to an RRSP.

Such a retiring allowance may be received by a dependant or relative of the taxpayer after his or her death or by his or her estate and tax may also be deferred by transferring eligible amounts to his or her RRSP.

The maximum amount of a retiring allowance that can be transferred on a tax-free basis to an RPP or RRSP is $3,500 for each calendar year the employee was employed by the employer paying the amount. If the employee was a member of the employer's pension plan or deferred profit sharing plan (DPSP), the maximum is reduced to $2,000 for each year the employer's contributions to such plans had vested in the employee. Only $2,000 a year for each year of service after 1988 may be transferred to an RRSP.

Any amount of a retiring allowance not transferred to either type of plan must be included in income in the year of receipt and will be taxed at your marginal rate. If your retiring allowance is significant in relation to other sources of income, the alternative minimum tax may apply where the retiring allowance is transferred to an RRSP. If the alternative minimum tax does apply, it may be recovered in one or more of the seven taxation years following the taxation year it is payable, depending on an individual's income and deductions in those years.

Bear in mind that RRSPs must be matured in the year you turn 71. You will have no opportunity to defer tax with an RRSP if you are 72 or older when you receive the retiring allowance, as the retiring allowance cannot be transferred to a spousal plan.

You may want to arrange for your employer to transfer your retiring allowance directly to your RRSP, in which case no tax need be withheld. If you receive the amount directly from your employer and then make the transfer, your employer must withhold tax, which you can then claim as a refund on your tax return.

Contributions to Deferred Profit Sharing Plans (DPSPs)

Your employer may be making deductible contributions to a DPSP on your behalf. The maximum employer contribution for 1990 is the lesser of 20 per cent of the employee's remuneration and $3,500 less any amount contributed by the employer on behalf of that employee to a registered pension plan. Under the retirement saving reform, the total employer contribution will be limited to the lesser of 18 per cent of the employee's remuneration and the following amounts:

1991	$6,250
1992	6,750
1993	7,250
1994	7,750

The maximum figure of $7,750 will be indexed beginning in 1995 according to increases in the average wage. DPSPs must provide that the employer make a contribution based on company profits, but no contribution need be made in a loss year. A DPSP does not permit any type of past service contribution.

Employee Contributions. The pension reform will prohibit employee contributions to a DPSP after 1989.

Receipts from DPSPs. Amounts received from DPSPs must be included in income, except for capital amounts contributed by the employee. Most plans allow for payment of taxable amounts to be spread over a maximum of ten years, or it is possible before reaching age 71 to purchase an annuity for life whose guaranteed terms, if any, cannot exceed 15 years. Employee contributions may be withdrawn at any time. DPSP proceeds also can be deferred by transferring them into an RPP, an RRSP, or another eligible DPSP.

Unpaid Amounts from Transactions Outstanding for Two Previous Taxation Years

In non-arm's length situations, this provision generally applies in two ways: if you owe money for outlays or expenses incurred, other than remuneration (see below), that have been deducted from income; or if you have not been paid for goods or services you have provided. The situation often occurs between a corporation and a controlling shareholder.

If you have incurred an expense in the 1987 taxation year that was deducted from your income and that remains owing to a related taxpayer (creditor) during your 1988 and 1989 taxation years, such an unpaid amount will be added back to your income in the 1990 taxation year, unless you file Form T2047 by April 30, 1991, which, in effect, deems that the unpaid amount is paid on January 1, 1990, and that the creditor loans the amount (net of any tax required to be withheld) back to you at the same time. A corporation would have to file Form T2047 within six months of the end of its 1990 taxation year. In each case, the creditor must also sign the form.

If the election is not made and the amount is added back to the debtor's income in the 1990 taxation year, the subsequent payment of the unpaid amount would not be a deductible expense, although it would, of course, be included in the recipient's income in the year of receipt. It is therefore important to avoid this penalty.

Where both parties are on the accrual basis and the amount has been included in the income of the creditor, Revenue Canada's practice is not to invoke this provision.

While there is a procedure for late filing, a penalty requires 25 per cent of the unpaid amount to be included in the debtor's income.

Unpaid Remuneration to Anyone

An employer is not allowed a deduction for remuneration expense in the year incurred if the amount remains unpaid to the employee more than 179 days after the year end of the employer. Deferring remuneration therefore provides only a limited benefit. The employer will receive the deduction in the year the remuneration is actually paid. This provision applies whether or not the employer and employee are related. Remuneration expense does not include reasonable amounts for vacation or holiday pay, or deferred amounts under a salary deferral arrangement (SDA).

The salary deferral arrangement rules (see below) do not affect remuneration amounts paid within the 180-day limit. Thus, for the year the remuneration is earned, employees will not have to include a benefit in income for tax purposes equal to the unpaid amount.

Salary Deferral Arrangements, Retirement Compensation Arrangements, and Employee Benefit Plans

Salary Deferral Arrangements. The rules concerning salary deferral arrangements were introduced to prevent abuses prevalent with respect to employee benefit plans.

A salary deferral arrangement is defined as a funded or unfunded plan involving an employee and employer under which the employee has postponed the receipt of his or her remuneration beyond the end of a year and it is reasonable to consider that one of the main purposes for the postponement is to defer the tax payable by the employee in respect of salary or wages for services rendered by him or her in the year or a preceding year. A variety of plans are excluded from the definition, including registered pension plans and other registered plans, certain benefit plans such as group sickness or accident insurance plans, plans to defer the salary of certain professional athletes, plans to provide funds for the education of workers, three-year bonus plans, and self-funded leave of absence plans. Also excluded are plans where certain conditions must be met for the eventual payment of the deferred amounts and there is substantial risk that the conditions will not be satisfied. (For example, the employee must exceed stringent sales targets.)

The rules regarding salary deferral arrangements do not apply to plans in existence on February 26, 1986, where amounts have been deferred in respect of services rendered after June 1986 if the employee is legally obligated to defer receipt of such amounts pursuant to an agreement in writing entered into before February 26, 1986, and if the employee cannot cancel or avoid the obligation.

Under the salary deferral arrangement rules, a right to receive deferred amounts, whether funded or not, must be recognized for tax purposes on the accrual basis and must be included in the employment income of the employee in the year the amount is earned, even if the amount is received at a later date. The employer will receive a deduction for the amount in that year. However, interest or other amounts paid by the employer in respect of the deferred salary will be treated as employment income in the year earned. For this reason, SDAs are excluded from the interest accrual rules. If a person besides the employee has a right to receive the deferred salary, these rules still come into play.

Retirement Compensation Arrangements (RCA). An RCA is generally any plan or arrangement established after October 8, 1986, under which payments are made by an employer or former employer (or related person) of a taxpayer to a custodian in connection with benefits to be provided to the taxpayer or others on the retirement, loss of office, etc. of the taxpayer. Certain arrangements are specifically excluded from the definition, such as registered pension plans, employee profit sharing plans and DPSPs, RRSPs, group sickness and accident insurance plans, certain plans established for professional athletes and officials, and SDAs.

Essentially, contributions to an RCA are deductible by the employer when made but are subject to a refundable 50 per cent withholding tax. This tax is refunded when payments are made from the RCA and included in the recipient's income. Income earned in the RCA on the contributions is also subject to a 50 per cent tax that is refundable when payments are made to beneficiaries. Any income from an RCA is not taxable to the recipient until actually received.

The RCA rules are applicable for Quebec tax purposes, except for the 50 per cent tax on amounts contributed and on the income generated by the plan.

Employee Benefit Plans. In the unlikely event that a deferral plan does not fall within the definition of a salary deferral arrangement or a retirement compensation arrangement, it is likely that the plan is an employee benefit plan (EBP), in which case the employer will not receive a deduction for amounts deferred. (Prior to the introduction of the SDA rules, employee benefit plans were frequently used to defer the salary of employees who worked for non-taxable employers, such as government, non-profit organizations, or companies in a loss position.) Under such a plan, a portion of the employee's salary is placed with a custodian. The employer receives no deduction for amounts directed to the custodian, and the employee is not taxed on such amounts until they are actually received. Investment income earned on the deferred amounts is taxed in the hands of the plan, or in the hands of the employee or employer.

This is the case for self-funded leave of absence arrangements, under which an employee may defer up to one-third of his or her salary each year for up to six years. The deferred amount must be included in the income of the employee for tax purposes in the seventh year.

Shareholder Loans

If a shareholder or a person related to the shareholder receives a loan or incurs any type of indebtedness (other than loans described below) from the shareholder's corporation or a related corporation, and the amount is not repaid by the end of the lender's following taxation year, the amount of the loan is included in the debtor's income in the year the loan was made. This may necessitate amending that year's income tax return. If the amount is included in income and is repaid at a later date, it is deductible from income in the year of repayment. However, a series of loans and repayments would not qualify for this treatment.

You should ensure that you have sufficient income to absorb any deduction due to repayment of such a loan.

There are four other exceptions to the rules requiring a loan to be included in income:

- when the creditor lends the money as part of its ordinary business;
- when loans are made to employees of the creditor or their spouses to enable or assist them to purchase a dwelling for their own habitation;
- when loans are made to employees of the creditor to enable or assist them to purchase an automobile to be used by them while performing the duties of their employment;
- when a corporate creditor loans funds to employees to enable or assist them to purchase, from the corporation or a

related corporation, fully paid treasury shares of the corporation to be held by them for their own benefit.

This last provision does not provide for the employee to purchase shares from any other shareholder; rather, they must be purchased directly from the corporation.

In each of the four cases, bona fide arrangements must be in place at the time the loan is made for repayment of the loan or indebtedness within a reasonable period.

The taxable benefit rules regarding imputed interest on low-interest or interest-free employee loans apply for the most part to all types of shareholder loans and indebtedness. However, home purchase and home relocation loan rules are not applicable to shareholder loans unless the shareholder is an employee and the loan was received because of the borrower's status as an employee.

Advances to shareholders during the year in anticipation of dividend payments are considered to be indebtedness in respect of which the imputed interest taxable benefit rules apply.

The act under which a corporation is incorporated may contain rules regarding the loaning of money to employees, officers, directors, and shareholders of the corporation; therefore, reference should be made to that act before any such loan is made.

4. Income Splitting

Income splitting occurs when income that normally would be taxed entirely in your hands is taxed in the hands of both you and another person with a lower marginal tax rate, for example, your spouse or children. If the difference in marginal tax rates is 20 per cent, the family's tax saving is $200 for every $1,000 of income transferred to the lower-rate individual (assuming the transfer does not bump the transferee into a higher tax bracket).

However, the government is aware of this benefit, and the Income Tax Act contains provisions, called the attribution rules, that are designed to discourage income splitting. These rules have been tightened considerably in recent years and have the effect of attributing the income back to you, so that it is taxed in your hands, despite the fact that you have not personally received it. These are dangerous tax traps to be avoided whenever possible.

Transfers to Your Spouse or Minor Children

The attribution rules apply if an individual loans or transfers property to, or for the benefit of, a spouse (or future spouse) or certain minors, or a trust established for such a person. The attribution rules apply to minors (under age 18) with whom the individual does not deal at arm's length (child, grandchild, brother, sister, brother-in-law, sister-in-law, etc.) and to an individual's niece or nephew. Property includes money, shares, bonds, a right of any kind, a home, land, etc.

If the attribution rules apply, income (or losses) from loaned or transferred property, or from property substituted for it, is not taxed in the hands of the recipient spouse, related minor, or niece or nephew, but is included in the income of the individual who made the loan or transfer. It is, in effect, the net income or loss from the property that is attributed to the lender or transferor. Although the attribution rules apply to property income and losses, they do not apply to most business income generated by the loaned or transferred property. See "Business Income" below.

The attribution rules also apply to capital gains and losses realized by a spouse on loaned or transferred property or substituted property. There is no attribution of capital gains or losses realized by a minor (under age 18 throughout the taxation year), except in certain cases involving farm property that has been previously given preferential tax treatment.

Capital gains are attributable only to the transferor for transfers occurring after 1971, whereas income, which does not include capital gains, is attributable no matter when the transfer was made. Thus, a capital gain arising from property transferred before 1972 is not attributable, but any income earned on that property, such as dividends, is attributable to the transferor. For loaned property (or property substituted for it), there is attribution of capital gains for loans made after May 22, 1985, and for dispositions after 1987 where the loan was outstanding on May 22, 1985.

Although the income or gain is attributed for tax purposes, these amounts still legally belong to the spouse or minor. Generally speaking, there is no attribution of income earned on attributed income, although there is an exception where the attributed income is a stock dividend.

The attribution rules apply where there has been a transfer of property. The word "transfer" has been interpreted very broadly. For example, it includes a gift or may include a sale at fair market value. The rules apply where there has been a loan or transfer of property "either directly or indirectly, by means of a trust or by any other means whatever, to or for the benefit of a person" who is a related minor, niece, nephew, or the spouse of a lender or transferor. For example, the rules apply to situations where an individual loans or transfers property to a trust, the beneficiaries of which include his spouse or related minors, nieces and nephews (see below). Special rules also apply where property has been loaned or transferred to a corporation.

For there to be attribution of income (or loss), the spouse or minor child must initially have an amount included in income (except in certain corporate situations). For example, if property is transferred to a trust for the benefit of minor children and the income from the property is taxed in the trust, there is no attribution of income. (Note, however, that all of the income of an inter vivos trust is taxed at the highest personal tax rate and no advantage would be gained. In Quebec, the income is taxed at the higher of 20 per cent, or the regular tax rate for individuals.) If the income is paid or payable to the children from the trust and is therefore included in their income, the attribution rules will apply. However, a net loss suffered by a trust cannot be allocated to beneficiaries and, consequently, there can never be attribution of trust losses.

The attributed income retains its character (except in corporate attribution situations). For example, if an individual loans funds to his spouse, who invests the funds in preferred shares, any dividends, capital gains, or capital losses on the preferred shares will be attributed back to the individual, who will treat the amounts as dividends (subject to the gross-up and credit mechanism), capital gains (eligible for the lifetime capital gains exemption), or capital losses.

Trusts. If the attributed income is earned through a trust, special rules apply to determine how much trust income of a designated beneficiary (i.e., the spouse, minor child, minor niece or nephew) is attributed. These rules will produce different results depending on whether all or only a portion of the income earned by the trust is from "loaned or transferred property", or whether there is more than one designated beneficiary.

If Mr. A and Mrs. A each decides to contribute funds to the same trust that includes their minor child as a beneficiary, the income of that minor would seem to be attributed to both Mr. A and Mrs. A, which would lead to double taxation. However, if each parent created a separate trust, only the income of one trust would be attributed back to the parent who created it.

If you have established a trust for a spouse or minor child and either loaned or transferred property to the trust, you should review your situation to ensure you do not inadvertently stumble into unfortunate tax complications.

Substituted Property. The attribution rules apply not only to loaned or transferred property but also to property that is substituted for the loaned or transferred property. For example, if an individual loans funds to a spouse, who uses the funds to acquire preferred shares, the shares are substituted property and the attribution rules would apply to the income from, and capital gains or losses on, the shares. If the preferred shares were sold and the funds were used to acquire bonds, the bonds would be substituted property to which the attribution rules would apply.

The definition of substituted property states that a stock dividend received on a share will be considered property substituted for that share. Accordingly, the attribution rules will apply to any income earned (and in the case of a spouse, any gains realized) on a stock dividend that was received as income on loaned or transferred or substituted property. As noted below, this is contrary to the general rule that there is no attribution of income on attributed income. Stock dividends are, in most cases, now treated the same as cash dividends for tax purposes.

No Attribution. In the case of a related minor, attribution generally ceases the year the child turns 18, but see "Property Loaned to Non-Arm's Length Party" below. In the case of a spouse, attribution ceases upon divorce or when the spouses are living separate and apart by reason of marriage breakdown. The transferor/lender spouse must file an election (which is a joint election with the transferee/borrower) for the attribution of capital gains not to occur after the breakdown of a marriage. Attribution also stops when a lender or transferor dies or ceases to be resident in Canada.

In addition, income from fair market value (FMV) transfers (i.e., sales) and loans is not subject to attribution. The attribution rules may not apply to a loan if:

- interest is charged on the loan at a reasonable rate or at the rate prescribed for income tax purposes at the time the loan was made; and
- the interest payable for each year is paid within 30 days after the end of that year.

In the case of a transfer, there is no attribution if:

- the FMV of the transferred property does not exceed the FMV of the consideration received by the transferor on the transfer;
- where the consideration received includes debt, the conditions listed above for an exempt loan are met; and
- where the property is transferred to a spouse, the transferor elects in his or her return for the year in which the property is transferred not to have the tax-deferred rollover provisions apply (applicable to any taxable capital gain).

Property Loaned to Non-Arm's Length Party

Since 1989, income attribution applies when an individual loans property to another individual with whom he or she does not deal at arm's length and it is reasonable to consider that one of the main reasons for the loan is to reduce or avoid tax on income from the property (or property substituted for it) by causing such income to be included in the income of the other individual.

This new application of attribution rules covers loans between individuals who are connected by blood relationship, marriage or adoption. Parents, spouses and even adult children are affected. The outright transfer of property to a non-arm's length individual is, however, not affected. Like the regular attribution rules, it is only the net income or loss from the property that would be attributed.

The typical situation covered by this rule is a low-interest or no-interest loan made to your adult child. There is an exemption from the new rule if you charge a commercial rate of interest. If, however, the rate of interest is less than both the prescribed interest rate for income tax purposes (announced quarterly) and the rate that arm's length parties would have agreed to under similar circumstances when the loan was made, income attribution will still apply. It will also apply if the interest on the loan is not paid within 30 days after the end of each year. Attribution applies only where the loan is invested by the debtor. If the debtor spends the funds for a non-investment purpose (e.g., paying tuition fees), there is no income to attribute.

Corporate Attribution Rules

These rules apply to loans and transfers made after October 27, 1986. In very broad terms, they operate as follows: if an individual loans or transfers property to a corporation and one of the main purposes of the loan or transfer may reasonably be considered to be to reduce the individual's income and to benefit a "designated person" (a spouse or certain minors if they own at least 10 per cent of any class of shares of the corporation) in respect of the individual, unless the individual receives (as a minimum) an annual prescribed return on the debt or shares received on the loan or transfer of property, there will be deemed attribution of interest income to the individual lender or transferor.

The corporate attribution rules do not apply to any period during which the corporation is a small business corporation (SBC). An SBC is basically a Canadian-controlled private corporation (CCPC) that primarily carries on an active business in Canada. A public corporation cannot be an SBC, nor can CCPCs that hold portfolio investments or carry on a personal services business (i.e., an incorporated employee).

When you remember the broad meaning given to the word transfer (which would include a sale at FMV), you can appreciate how broad the rules are. The following comments highlight some potential problems:

- The attribution rules can apply where the shareholders of the corporation to which an individual has loaned or transferred property include the individual's spouse, certain mi-

nors, or a partnership or trust in which the spouse or a minor is, respectively, a member or a beneficiary if the spouse or the minor (whether directly or through a trust or partnership) owns at least 10 per cent of any class of shares of the corporation or a related corporation.
- Unlike the normal attribution rules discussed above, the spouse or a minor need not receive income for the corporate attribution rules to apply.

Corporate attribution rules do not apply when the shares of the corporation are held in trust, and under the terms of the trust, the individual may not receive any of the capital or income of the trust while he or she is a designated person (spouse, related minor, niece or nephew).

Getting Around the Attribution Rules

The attribution rules are now much broader and more complex than in the past, and attempts at income splitting now give new meaning to the phrase "a splitting headache".

Many of the old techniques (for example, loans to spouses and trusts for minor children) for splitting large amounts of income quickly are no longer available. However, new opportunities (such as a sale at fair market value) are now available.

A variety of planning opportunities are discussed below. Generally, it has become difficult, if not impossible, to have large amounts of income taxed in your spouse's or children's hands rather than in your hands over a short period of time. It is now important to begin your income splitting program as early as possible and continually update it. The discussion below assumes that you have and will continue to have a higher tax rate than your spouse and children.

Business Income

The attribution rules do not generally apply to business income earned by your spouse or child with transferred or loaned funds. Thus, if you give your spouse or child money to finance a personally run business or invest in a partnership in which the spouse or child actively participates, income from that business should not be attributed to you; however, any capital gain that arises on disposition of the business by your spouse would be attributed to you. There is no attribution of capital gains earned by your minor child except where the property is farm property which previously received preferential tax treatment. The attribution rules also should not apply if you and your spouse operate a business as a bona fide partnership.

If you have loaned or transferred property to a person which is an interest in a partnership, that person's share of the business income of the partnership may be considered as income from property (and not income from business) for purposes of the attribution rules and may therefore be attributed back to you.

This provision will apply where the person is a "specified member" of the partnership. This occurs where the person:

- was a limited partner of the partnership during the fiscal period in which the income arose; and
- was neither actively engaged in the activities of the partnership nor carried on a business similar to that of the partnership, otherwise than as a member of the partnership, on a regular, continuous and substantial basis throughout the period.

For example, you give or loan your spouse $100,000 that is used to acquire an interest in a limited partnership. Under the attribution rules, if your spouse is only a passive investor and if your spouse's share of the partnership income is $10,000 in 1990, that $10,000 will be added to your 1990 income, not to that of your spouse.

Interest on Interest

The attribution rules do not mean that you should abandon the idea of giving or loaning your spouse or children funds to earn investment income. The fact that interest on interest is not attributed can prove to be significant in the long run. For example, if you give your spouse $20,000, which is invested to earn 12 per cent annually over the next ten years with the interest paid annually and reinvested at this same rate, then only the simple interest of $24,000 (12 per cent of $20,000 = $2,400 times 10 years) will be attributed to you. Interest on interest of $18,117, over and above the simple interest of $24,000, will be earned over the ten-year period, if the annual interest of $2,400 is reinvested at 12 per cent, and it will be taxed in your spouse's hands, not in yours.

Spousal Registered Retirement Savings Plans

With the tightening up of the attribution rules, taxpayers should definitely consider making use of spousal RRSPs. Details on how spousal RRSPs operate are contained in Chapter 6.

The principal advantage of contributing to a spousal RRSP is the achievement of future income splitting since the attribution rules do not apply. The annuity or registered retirement income fund (RRIF) payments eventually arising from the spousal RRSP are taxable in the hands of your spouse, and not in your hands.

If there is some chance that you will need to withdraw RRSP funds in the near future, you should ensure that any spousal RRSP contributions are made to a separate plan. Any funds withdrawn from your spouse's RRSP can be attributed to you if you contributed to this RRSP during the year or during the two years preceding the withdrawal. You should remember that amounts contributed to a spousal RRSP belong to your spouse.

If you contribute to your spouse's RRSP, you should make the payment directly to the trustee and have it receipted to you, so that you can prove that you made the payment.

Paying Spouse's Taxes

If your income is higher than your spouse's, you might consider paying your spouse's taxes as another method of effectively transferring funds to your spouse. This amount would be considered a gift by you to your spouse. Of course, no income would be earned on the amount since it is used to pay taxes and therefore, there would be no attribution. Your spouse could then invest the funds that otherwise would have gone to pay his or her taxes, and any income earned on these funds would not be attributed back to you. This arrangement would not work to the extent that the spouse's taxes were deducted at source by an employer.

Paying Family Expenses

If both spouses are earning income but one spouse will continually have a higher tax rate than the other, the higher-income spouse should consider paying all or most of the family expenses while the lower-income spouse invests all or most of his or her earnings. The income generated from these investments will be taxed at a lower rate.

Paying Your Spouse or Child a Salary

You may pay your spouse or child a salary for work performed in your unincorporated business and deduct the salary in determining your income from the business. The amount will be taxed in your spouse's or child's hands, not in your hands. The salary or wages paid must be reasonable in relation to the duties performed. Your spouse or child may then be in a position to contribute to the Canada Pension Plan and also to an RRSP.

Spousal Business Partnerships

Even though you may pay a salary to your spouse, there may be reasons why you want to establish that the business is actually a partnership, thereby entitling the spouse to a share of partnership profits. This situation is common in farm operations, but may apply to any type of business. You should establish a properly documented partnership agreement detailing the profit-sharing arrangements and ownership of assets of the business. If Revenue Canada considers the allocation of the partnership income to be unreasonable, it will change it to an allocation that it considers reasonable in the circumstances.

If the spouse's capital contribution to the business is significant, a spousal partnership generally will be more advantageous than paying the spouse a salary. This could permit a larger share of the business profits to be recognized by the spouse than would be the case if the spouse were paid a reasonable salary for duties performed.

In situations where, for example, you are operating a sideline business that has a reasonable expectation of medium-term profit, it may be advantageous to be able to pay your spouse a reasonable salary, thereby creating a loss in the business for a given year. This may be the case if you have other sources of income against which the losses can be applied.

If you cannot establish a spousal partnership, you could consider incorporating the business, and your spouse could participate by owning shares acquired with his or her own funds.

Transfers at Fair Market Value

You may elect to transfer property to your spouse and receive fair market value consideration for it. Under certain conditions, the attribution rules will not apply, and future income and capital gains will be taxed in your spouse's hands. For capital property, this means that you would have to recognize any accrued capital gains or losses at the time of the transfer. Such capital gains are eligible for your lifetime capital gains exemption.

If property with unrealized capital losses is transferred at fair market value, the superficial loss rules come into play, and you will be denied the capital loss if the property is still owned by your spouse 31 days after the transfer.

Some taxpayers will be taking advantage of these spousal transfer rules to realize gains eligible for the lifetime capital gains exemption. By transferring capital property with accrued gains from one spouse to the other at fair market value, eligible gains are realized, but ownership of the property remains in the family. This also allows you to avoid paying a broker's commission on the sale of securities that you want to continue to hold.

Gift Interest Expense to Your Spouse

Income must be earned or capital gains realized on funds transferred or gifted to your spouse for the attribution rules to be applied. Hence, there is no attribution if no income is earned on the transferred funds. Similarly, if you give your spouse funds to pay the interest on a loan made by you to your spouse, there should be no attribution in respect of the amount gifted for the interest expense, nor attribution of the net income earned by the spouse from the loaned funds. Of course, the loan must be a bona fide loan, interest must be charged at the lesser of the prescribed rate for tax purposes and commercial rates, and the interest payable must be paid within 30 days of the year end.

You must include the interest paid by the spouse in income for tax purposes, but you will benefit because the spouse's investment income will compound much more quickly since it is not being diluted annually by an interest payment on the loan.

Using Transferred Funds for Leverage

The income or capital gains earned on funds borrowed by your spouse on a commercial basis with no guarantee by you is not attributable. Thus, if you were considering borrowing for investment purposes, you might consider transferring funds to your spouse which would enable him or her to borrow. For example, you might give your spouse $25,000 and he or she would then borrow $75,000. The spouse then buys $100,000 worth of securities that would be lodged as collateral with the lending institution in lieu of your guarantee. In this situation, only 25 per cent of any net income or capital gains earned ($25,000/$100,000) would be attributed to you.

Locking in the Best Rate on Spousal Loans

If you intend to loan funds to your spouse, you will generally charge interest at the prescribed rate (the rate applicable to late tax payments and overpayments of tax), which usually will be lower than commercial lending rates. The prescribed rate is set each quarter based on 90-day Treasury Bill yields of the first month of the preceding quarter. Thus, the rate for any quarter is known about two months in advance. Before locking in the interest rate on a spousal loan for any longer than three months, you should determine the direction in which the prescribed rate will move in the next quarter. If the rate is expected to increase, you might consider setting the term of the loan for an extended period if you do not expect rates to fall again. If the rate is expected to decline, you should keep the loan on a variable rate basis.

Optional Payment of Interest

Interest on a spousal loan does not have to be actually paid by the spouse until 30 days after the year end. If any amount less than the minimum amount of interest remains unpaid after that date, the attribution rules apply. Thus, you might consider loaning your spouse funds at the beginning of the year. Depending on how the spouse's investments performed, you could decide near the end of January in the following year whether or not to pay the interest. If the investments did well, the spouse would pay the interest and the loan would remain outstanding. If the investments did poorly, the interest would not be paid and the amount attributed to you would be limited to the actual yield of the investment.

One drawback to this planning is that if interest is not paid on the loan, attribution will apply in all future years on this particular transfer of property, even though the spouse may pay the interest on the loan in a subsequent year. The only solution could be for the spouse to sell the investments and repay the loan. Then you could loan new funds to your spouse at some future date.

Professional Management Companies

Professional management companies are popular because the attribution rules do not apply to small business corporations. Such companies are generally set up by professionals such as doctors or dentists who are not allowed by their governing bodies to incorporate. The company, which is owned by the spouse and/or children of the professional, provides services to the professional and is paid a fee, usually about 15 per cent above the cost of the services. Such services could include the rental of equipment and facilities, the services of assistants, and bookkeeping, secretarial and administrative types of services. When arranging such a corporation, professional advice should be sought to ensure the company will not be considered a personal services business that has certain limitations or expenses and affects the rate of tax the corporation will pay.

If it is incorporated, such a business is considered to be a small business corporation and no attribution of income will occur if the professional loans or sells assets to the corporation and your spouse or children are shareholders. If the management business is unincorporated, which is generally not advisable, and assets are transferred to the spouse and used to earn business income, there would be no attribution of that income.

Granting Spouse an Option to Purchase

One problem with selling capital property to your spouse or loaning funds to him or her for a purchase is that the spouse's investments may not earn any or enough income to pay the interest expense each year. For example, you may sell speculative shares to your spouse and take back a note with interest payable annually. However, these shares may not currently be paying dividends, even though they are increasing in value and promise to realize large capital gains when they are eventually sold. Your spouse has no other source of income to use for the interest payments on the loan, but the interest must be paid by the spouse with his or her own funds for the attribution rules not to apply (if several other planning techniques discussed above are ignored).

One way around the problem may be to grant your spouse an option to purchase your shares on or before some future date at the fair market value of the shares on the date the option was granted. For example, assume that you own 1,000 shares of X Corp that you purchased for $3 and now are worth $12. You sell an option to purchase these shares for $12 each to your spouse for, say, $1 per share, which is the fair market value of the option at that time. The spouse would pay $1 per share for the option with his or her own funds. The option will expire in seven years.

Assume that the shares increase in value to $20 after two years and your spouse exercises the option. You deliver the shares to your spouse and realize a gain of $9 a share since he or she pays you $12 for each share (not including the $1 per share option payment). The option froze the fair market value of thc shares to you at $12. Your spouse can immediately sell the shares for $20 each and realize a gain of $7 a share ($20 minus $12 minus option price of $1). Since you sold the shares to your spouse for your fair market value ($12) and received fair market value consideration for them ($12 cash each), there is no attribution of the $7 gain realized by your spouse.

If the shares decline in value, your spouse would simply let the option expire at the end of the seven-year period and you would still own the shares.

Emigrating from Canada

Income and capital gains earned by your spouse on property transferred or loaned by you is not subject to the attribution rules if you, the transferor or lender, become a non-resident of Canada. Thus, if you have large gains that will not be exempted under the lifetime $100,000 capital gains exemption, if your spouse has all or a portion of his or her exemption available, and if you both intend to take up residence outside Canada, you might consider timing the transfer of property to your spouse in such a way as to avoid the attribution of any accrued capital gains.

For example, assume that you and your spouse plan to retire to Florida early in 1991. You own shares with unrealized taxable capital gains of $50,000, but you have used up your capital gains exemption. However, your spouse has $80,000 of his or her exemption left. Just before the end of 1990, you transfer the shares to your spouse at your cost. You then move to Florida on or before December 31. Your spouse remains a resident of Canada and sells the shares early in January and realizes the gain. Shortly thereafter, he or she leaves the country.

The gain is realized by your spouse after you have taken up residence in Florida so there should be no attribution of the capital gain. Unfortunately, it is not a simple matter to determine exactly when an individual gives up residence in one country and takes up residence in another. Revenue Canada may argue that, at least for tax purposes, you did not give up your Canadian residence until after your spouse sold the shares.

A Word of Caution

A number of the above suggestions are "aggressive", i.e., the tax authorities may not take kindly to taxpayers using them. If you are considering any of these aggressive techniques, you should consult with your professional advisors to identify any possible disadvantages. In many cases, you will not be worse off if the plan is scuttled somehow or other, since the attributed income or capital gain would have been realized in your hands in any case.

Transfers to Minors and the Attribution Rules

Rules similar to the spousal attribution rules apply to income from property transferred or loaned to certain minors. The attribution rules apply where the minor is a niece or nephew or where the minor is not an arm's length party, for example, the minor is a child, grandchild, brother, or sister of the transferor. As well, rules similar to the attribution rules apply where property is loaned to any non-arm's length person such as an adult child. The attribution rules do not apply to capital gains realized by anyone other than a spouse. However, since the transfer of property to a related person must be at fair market value, unless specific exemptions apply, the transferor may have to recognize a capital gain at the time of the transfer.

The introduction of the lifetime capital gains exemption may make the gifting of capital property to children less attractive to many taxpayers, since there is little point in giving up ownership and control of an asset if there are no tax advantages. However, such a gift will permit your own and your spouse's lifetime capital gains exemptions to be used up more slowly if your children realize capital gains that would otherwise be recognized by you or your spouse.

Many of the planning techniques discussed above concerning the splitting of income (primarily interest and dividends) with your spouse also apply to splitting income with your children. Where loans or sales to a minor are involved, you should consider using a trust to avoid any future legal problems. (Special legal considerations are involved if a trust with minor children as beneficiaries is created in Quebec.)

Family Allowance Payments

The most common method of generating income that is taxable in the hands of a child is to place family allowance cheques for that child in the child's own investment vehicle, such as a savings account, bonds, investment certificates, etc. The income earned on these funds will not be attributed back to you.

Registered Education Savings Plans (RESPs)

Although Registered Education Savings Plans (RESPs) have been around for a number of years, they have not been all that popular in the past, because contributions to an RESP are not deductible for tax purposes, and other arrangements were more attractive. More interest is now being shown in such plans, especially as a means for grandparents to fund their grandchildren's education while retaining the flexibility to withdraw the capital should they need the cash.

The main purpose of an RESP is to fund the post-secondary education of an individual ("the beneficiary") by allowing funds to accumulate tax-free within the RESP. A subscriber would contribute funds to an RESP and specify the beneficiary. Essentially, the only payments that can be made from an RESP are educational assistance payments to the designated beneficiary and a tax-free refund of contributions to the subscriber. If the designated beneficiary does not receive any post-secondary education, the income earned in the RESP on the contributions is forfeited. However, the terms of the plan may allow a change to be made in the beneficiary named, and some plans permit multiple beneficiaries to be named. Neither the subscriber nor the RESP is taxable on the accumulating income. On the future payment of such income to the beneficiary, the amounts would be included in the income of the beneficiary in the year received. The beneficiary would then be able to claim the tuition fee tax credit to lessen the tax impact of such income inclusion.

There are very few legislative restrictions or conditions imposed on an RESP. Most plan terms are stipulated by the promoter, so read the promoter's literature and the contract carefully.

Maintaining a Dependant's Status

If the child has qualifying "earned income", a contribution could bemade to an RRSP on behalf of the child. This will lower the child's income and, together with tuition fees and other deductions or credits, may place the child in a dependent category, allowing the parent to claim the child as a dependant and/or to utilize a portion of the child's tuition fee and education tax credits.

Testamentary Planning

If your children are grown and have their own minor children, you might consider bequeathing funds in your will in trust to your grandchildren rather than your adult children. On your death, the funds would go in trust, with your children as trustees, to the minor grandchildren. There would be no attribution, since the attribution rules cease to apply on the death of the transferor. The grandchildren would earn income on the bequeathed funds and be taxed at a much lower rate than if their parents (your children) had earned the income. The parents could direct the trust to use the funds and income for the education costs of your grandchildren.

Farm Property Transfers

There is an exception where capital gains do not have to be recognized by the transferor on certain transfers to a child. A transfer during your lifetime of farm property to a child, grandchild, or great-grandchild may be made at any value between your adjusted cost base of the farming property and its fair market value. The child assumes a cost base equal to the transfer value and becomes liable for any capital gains on disposition. However, if the child disposes of the farming property, including farming assets, before the year he or she turns 18, any capital gain will be attributed to you.

A farm property is one of which substantially all the assets are used in farming. The property must be actively farmed by the transferor or any family member immediately before transfer, and the child must be a Canadian resident. Such a tax-deferred transfer is also allowed for an interest in a qualifying farm partnership and for shares of farm corporations.

A full $500,000 capital gains exemption is available on the disposition of qualified farm property, consisting of your regular $100,000 lifetime exemption plus an additional $400,000 exemption.

Unless you otherwise expect to use your exemption, your children will be better off (i.e., will have a smaller gain to realize eventually) if you transfer the property at a value above your cost and recognize all or a portion of any resulting gain that would be exempt under your lifetime capital gains exemption.

5. Personal Tax Credits

The Essentials

Unlike tax deductions, tax credits provide the same dollar benefit to each taxpayer claiming a particular credit because the credit is subtracted directly from the individual's tax payable. If, however, the individual has no tax payable from which the credit can be deducted, and the credit is not refundable, the value of the credit is lost.

From a tax planning point of view, it makes sense to be aware of the nature of the personal tax credits that exist, so that you can take advantage of them whenever possible. You should also be sensitive to some of the differences between the various credits. Note that the dollar values shown below represent the federal credits, which are deducted before computing provincial tax. (The Quebec system differs from that in the other provinces. See Chapter 12.) The total credits are therefore worth more than the federal-only dollar values shown below.

Single Status

The federal single status tax credit for individuals for 1990 is

$1,049. The federal credit is indexed annually according to increases in the Consumer Price Index above 3 per cent.

Married Status

In 1990, a person, who at any time in the year is a married person supporting a spouse with income of $514 or less, may claim a federal married tax credit of $874. The credit is reduced by 17 per cent of the spouse's income in excess of $514. Thus, no credit is available for a spouse whose income is $5,655 or more. If you live apart from your spouse at the end of the year by reason of marriage breakdown, any reduction in the married credit is calculated using your spouse's income for the year while married and not separated.

You may claim the credit for only one person. If you divorce and remarry in the same year, you won't double the credit. The married federal tax credit is indexed annually according to increases in the Consumer Price Index above 3 per cent.

Equivalent-to-Married

The equivalent-to-married tax credit may be claimed by individuals who support a wholly dependent person and are unmarried, or married but did not support or live with the spouse. The federal credit is $874 in 1990, reduced by 17 per cent of the dependant's income over $514. If the dependant's income is $5,655 or more, the credit is nil.

To claim the credit, you must, whether alone or in concert with others, maintain a self-contained domestic establishment in which you live and support the dependant. The dependant must be related to you, wholly dependent on you (or on you and certain others) for support, and must be resident in Canada, unless the dependant is your child. Except in the case of a parent or grandparent, the dependant must be either under 18 years of age or dependent by reason of mental or physical infirmity.

An individual may claim the equivalent-to-married credit in respect of only one other person, and no more than one individual may claim the credit for the same person or the same self-contained domestic establishment. If two or more individuals could otherwise claim the credit for the same dependant or the same self-contained domestic establishment, they must agree which one will claim the credit. In the absence of agreement, the credit will apparently not be allowed to any of them.

If you are entitled to claim the equivalent-to-married credit in respect of a person, neither you nor anyone else may claim a dependant tax credit in respect of that person. The equivalent-to-married federal tax credit is indexed annually according to increases in the Consumer Price Index above 3 per cent.

Dependants

Under Age 18. The federal tax credit for 1990 in respect of dependants under the age of 18 at any time in the year is $68 for each of the first two such dependants and $136 for each additional one, provided the income of each dependant does not exceed $2,570. The credit is reduced by 17 per cent of the dependant's income in excess of $2,570 and therefore disappears at the $2,969 income level ($3,368 for the third and succeeding children). "Dependant" means a child or grandchild of you or your spouse or, if resident in Canada at any time in the year, a parent, grandparent, brother, sister, uncle, aunt, niece, or nephew of you or your spouse.

Mental or Physical Infirmity. If a person is dependent on you by reason of mental or physical infirmity and is not under 18 years of age at any time in the year, you may claim a dependant tax credit of $257 in 1990, provided the dependant's income does not exceed $2,570. The credit is eroded if the dependant's income exceeds $2,570 and is reduced to nil if the dependant's income is $4,082 or more. "Dependant" has the same meaning as noted above for dependants under age 18.

General Rules on Credits for Dependants. Both the federal tax credit for dependants under age 18 and for mental or physical infirmity are indexed annually according to increases in the Consumer Price Index above 3 per cent.

A special rule provides that where family allowance is paid in respect of a dependant, you may claim a tax credit for that dependant only to the extent of the proportion of the family allowance paid in the year in respect of the dependant that was included in computing your income for the year. Generally, the spouse with the higher income is required to include family allowance payments in income.

If more than one individual is entitled to claim a dependant tax credit in respect of the same dependant, the total claimed by such individuals must not exceed the maximum allowed if only one individual were to make the claim. The tax department may allocate the total tax credit to the supporting individuals if they cannot agree on an allocation.

Age 65 and Over

Any taxpayer who has attained the age of 65 years before the end of 1990 may claim a $566 federal tax credit. This credit is not affected by the size or nature of your income. If you are unable to make full use of the credit, all or a portion of it can be transferred to your spouse. The federal credit is indexed annually according to increases in the Consumer Price Index above 3 per cent.

Mental or Physical Impairment

Persons with a severe and prolonged mental or physical impairment that has been certified by a medical doctor or optometrist may claim a federal tax credit in 1990 of $566. This federal credit is indexed annually according to increases in the Consumer Price Index above 3 per cent. Any unused portion of the credit may be transferred to a spouse.

Pension Income

If you have attained age 65 before the end of 1990, you may claim a maximum federal tax credit in respect of your pension income of $170, provided that income is at least $1,000. If it is less than $1,000, the maximum credit is 17 per cent of the pension income. A similar credit is available in respect of "qualified pension income" for taxpayers who have attained age 60 or receive certain disability or survivor's pensions.

Certain taxpayers younger than age 60 also may be eligible for this "qualified pension income" tax credit.

If you cannot make full use of your pension income tax credit, the unused portion may be transferred to your spouse. The pension tax credit is not subject to indexation and therefore remains at the level at which it was introduced in 1988.

CPP/QPP and Unemployment Insurance Credit

The federal CPP/QPP and UI tax credit is calculated as 17 per cent of CPP/QPP and UI payments for the year. Both the employee contribution and the "employer" amount that self-employed persons contribute to the CPP/QPP have been converted from a deduction to a credit.

For 1990, the maximum UI payments are $1,048.32 for employers and $748.80 for employees, while the maximum CPP payment is $574.20 by both employers and employees.

Charitable Donations

The federal tax credit on qualifying charitable donations is 17 per cent on the first $250 donated and 29 per cent on donations above $250. Thus, the total credit on a $1,000 donation for an individual in the top tax bracket in 1990 will be about $424:

Federal credit @ 17% on first $250 donated	$ 42.50
Federal credit @ 29% on excess - $750	217.50
Total federal credits	260.00
Surtax reduction	20.80
	280.80
Provincial tax reduction @ 55% of $260	143.00
Total tax reduction	$423.80

The annual limit on qualifying donations to charitable institutions is 20 per cent of net income. As well, any donation not claimed under the tax credit system still may be carried forward for five years. However, in the carryforward year, the 17 per cent rate applies to the first $250 of all donations against which a credit is claimed, including carryforward donations.

This may result in a small tax cost if you were not otherwise donating $250 in that year.

Claiming credit for $500 on one spouse's return (rather than each spouse claiming $250) saves tax because half the donation qualifies for the 29 per cent federal rate rather than 17 per cent rate.

Medical Expenses

The federal tax credit for 1990 in respect of medical expenses is 17 per cent of an amount that is calculated by subtracting from your total qualifying medical expenses the lesser of $1,542 and 3 per cent of your net income for the year. (The $1,542 amount is indexed annually according to increases in the Consumer Price Index above 3 per cent.) Receipts for the medical expenses must be filed when claiming the tax credit, and the expenses must not have previously been used. If the claimant dies within the year, the medical expenses must be paid within any 24-month period including the date of death. In any other case, they must be paid within any 12-month period ending in the taxation year. You should choose this 12-month period carefully, as it can affect the size of your tax credit. The Income Tax Act contains extensive provisions detailing the nature of expenditures that qualify as medical expenses.

Tuition Fees

The 1990 federal tuition fee tax credit is 17 per cent of eligible tuition fees paid in the year to a qualified post-secondary institution, or an institution certified by the Minister of Employment and Immigration, provided the total of such fees paid in the year to that institution exceeds $100. Special rules also extend the tax credit to eligible tuition fees paid by a full-time student enrolled at a university outside Canada, and to fees greater than $100 paid by a Canadian resident who commutes to an educational institution providing courses at the post-secondary level in the United States.

Only tuition fees paid in respect of the year are eligible to determine the tuition tax credit for that year. Where the tuition fees paid in a particular year cover the tuition required for an academic session extending beyond the particular year, they are eligible in determining the tuition tax credit for the year to which they relate. For example, where the session covered by the tuition fees extends from September of one year to April of the next year, the tuition tax credit is computed for each of those years as one-half of the total tuition fees paid multiplied by 17 per cent.

Any unused portion (up to $600) of the tuition fee tax credit and the education tax credit (see below) may be transferred for use by the student's spouse. If the spouse did not claim the student as a dependant and did not claim any of the student's unused tax credits that could have been transferred to the spouse, the student's supporting parent or grandparent may claim the student's unused tuition fee and education tax credits (to a maximum of $600). A prescribed form must be filed by the parent or grandparent making the claim.

Education

The federal education tax credit for 1990 is $10 for each month in the year during which you were a student in full-time attendance in a qualifying program at a designated educational institution. To claim the tax credit, you must file a certificate issued by the educational institution.

Refundable Sales and Child Tax Credits

These tax credits are federal credits only. There is no provincial "piggyback" effect to increase the value of these credits. For 1990, the sales tax credit is increased to $140 from $100 for each adult and to $70 from $50 for each dependent child under 19 years of age. The credit is reduced by 5 per cent of family net income in excess of $18,000.

The refundable federal child tax credit for 1990 is the total of two amounts: $575 per child plus $203 in respect of each eligible child under seven years of age at the end of the year. The $203 is reduced by 25 per cent of the amount of child care expenses claimed in respect of the child for the year. Both amounts that make up the child tax credit are indexed annually according to increases in the Consumer Price Index above 3 per cent.

The refundable child tax credit is reduced by 5 per cent of 1990 family income in excess of $24,769. If you qualify for the refundable child tax credit, be sure to file a tax return in order to claim it, even if you do not report taxable income. You must file the return to claim the credit.

Political Contributions

A federal tax credit is available for contributions to a registered political party or an officially nominated candidate in a federal election. The credit is based on the amount contributed and is calculated on a sliding scale, $500 being the maximum credit for any one taxation year.

Amount Contributed	Tax Credit Available
$ 1 - $ 100	75% of the contribution
$100 - $ 550	$75 plus 50% of excess over $100
$550 - $1,150	$300 plus one-third of excess over $550
Over $1,150	$500

All provinces and territories except Saskatchewan and Newfoundland also permit tax credits for political contributions, but the credit is deducted from provincial tax payable and contributions must be made to provincial political parties or associations, or to candidates standing for provincial election.

The tax credit in British Columbia, Manitoba, Nova Scotia, New Brunswick, Prince Edward Island and the Yukon Territory is calculated in the same manner as for federal purposes, the maximum credit being $500. In the Northwest Territories, the credit is 100 per cent of the first $100 contributed and 50 per cent of the excess over $100, to a maximum credit of $500. The maximum credit in Ontario is $750, calculated as 75 per cent of the first $200, 50 per cent of the next $600 and 33 1/3 per cent of the next $900. The maximum credit in Alberta is also $750, calculated as 75 per cent of the first $150 contributed, 50 per cent of the next $675, and 33 1/3 per cent of the next $900. In Quebec, the tax credit is calculated as 50 per cent of the first $280 contributed, the maximum credit being $140.

Official receipts must be filed with your tax return in order to receive the credit. Generally, political contributions must be made in the form of cash or other negotiable instruments (cheques, money orders, etc.). However, some of the provinces permit the contribution of goods or services under certain conditions.

Political contributions in excess of $1,150 ($900 in the Northwest Territories, $280 in Quebec, $1,725 in Alberta and $1,700 in Ontario) in any one taxation year will be lost for purposes of receiving the tax credit. If the tax credit exceeds your federal or provincial tax payable after the deduction of other credits, you are not allowed to claim a refund of tax or carry forward any excess credit to a future taxation year.

Planning for Your Contributions. If you are making a large contribution you should attempt to spread it over two years. This strategy is recommended in any case, since you will be able to take advantage of the larger credits available. For example, if you contribute $1,000 in one year, your credit (except in the Northwest Territories, Quebec, Ontario and Alberta) is $450. If you contribute $500 this year and $500 next year, your total credit is $550, giving you a $100 tax saving. This same technique should also be applied if both spouses earn taxable income, except the spouses would split their contribution in the year (i.e., each spouse would contribute $500, instead of one spouse contributing $1,000). Splitting the contribution is beneficial because the maximum percentage credit applies at lower contribution levels.

6. Saving for Retirement

Changes in Tax Assistance for Retirement Saving

Originally announced on October 9, 1986, the new system of tax assistance for retirement savings is finally law, with the major changes taking effect in 1991. Tax support is and will continue to be provided through tax-deductible contributions to registered savings plans, in which investment earnings can compound tax-free to fund the retirement income of plan members. These plans include Registered Pension Plans (RPPs), Registered Retirement Savings Plans (RRSPs), and Deferred Profit Sharing Plans (DPSPs), all of which will be significantly affected by the new legislation.

The basis of the new system is a uniform, comprehensive limit on tax-assisted savings of 18 per cent of an individual's earnings up to specified maximums. After a transition period, the maximum annual limits will reach $15,500 in 1995. According to the Government's estimates, contributions at this level will be sufficient to fund a pension of 2 per cent of pre-retirement earnings per year of service to a maximum of roughly $60,000 over a career of 35 years. Essentially, those are and will continue to be the limits imposed with respect to defined benefit pension plans. Beginning in 1995, both the contribution and pension limits will be indexed in accordance with the increase in the "average wage", in the same manner as the Canada and Quebec pension plans are adjusted.

Pension and deferred profit sharing plans will be closely regulated to ensure that they do not provide benefits in excess of stipulated limits and do not permit contributions greater than prescribed maximums. The aggregate value of the annual accumulation of retirement benefits in employer-sponsored plans will be measured for each individual member and will be restricted to a prescribed annual limit. Individual plan members will be able to supplement their employer plans by making RRSP contributions up to the specified limit. By 1995, individuals who are not members of RPPs or DPSPs will be entitled to contribute 18 per cent of their earnings, to a maximum of $15,500, to their RRSPs. In this fashion, integration of the uniform limit among the various types of retirement savings plans will be achieved.

THE BASICS

What Is an RRSP?

An RRSP is simply an investment vehicle in which you invest pre-tax employment or self-employed income within specific limits. No tax is paid on income earned in the RRSP. There are essentially two kinds of RRSPs. With the insurance type, typically an insurance company agrees to pay you an annuity of a certain amount beginning at a certain date if you make a lump-sum RRSP contribution or annual contributions to the RRSP of a specific amount until you are to begin receiving the annuity payments. The second, and more common type of RRSP, acts very much like a normal investment. You either deposit funds in an account that is registered as an RRSP investment (depositary RRSP) or you provide the RRSP issuer with funds and decide how these are to be invested (trusteed RRSP). Specific restrictions apply in both cases. Eventually, you arrange for these accumulated amounts to be paid back to you annually as retirement income.

As an investment vehicle for saving for retirement, RRSPs are in a class by themselves for most taxpayers. Enough can be contributed each year to fund most people's retirement needs and, provided certain conditions are met, no tax is paid on income earned in an RRSP until the funds are withdrawn, usually as a retirement income. As well, assuming that your tax rate does not change, an RRSP eliminates the tax on your net investment, which is the same as making a tax-free investment outside an RRSP (see below). RRSPs may also be used effectively for saving for a down payment on a home or for putting aside funds to see you through a year's sabbatical from your job.

Why Invest in an RRSP?

An RRSP is simply a contract or arrangement between you and another party, the issuer. In general terms, investments, such as guaranteed investment certificates or Canada Savings Bonds, are acquired by the issuer on your behalf.

There are four principal reasons for investing in an RRSP:

1. RRSPs Eliminate Tax. Assuming that your tax rate does not change over the years, an RRSP actually eliminates tax on your net investment. This concept should be at the heart of your decision when considering whether to use an RRSP.

The amount you contribute to an RRSP is deductible, within specified limits, from your income for tax purposes. Thus, the Government in effect participates in your investment. If you contribute $1,000 to an RRSP and your marginal tax rate is 40 per cent (the rate of tax levied on the last dollar of income you earn in the year), your tax bill is reduced by $400 (40 per cent of $1,000). Or put another way, the Government contributes $400 to your RRSP and you contribute $600 (your net investment) out of your after-tax earnings for a total of $1,000. If you do not contribute the $1,000 to the RRSP, you will pay tax of $400 and have only $600 left to invest outside the RRSP.

To prove that RRSPs eliminate tax, assume that you contribute the $1,000 to an RRSP: net investment of $600 plus your tax refund of $400. In 25 years, the $1,000 in the RRSP will grow to about $10,800 if it earns interest income at 10 per cent compounded annually. If tax is paid on the whole amount at the end of the 25-year period (normally you would defer tax longer by opting to receive an RRSP retirement income), you would have about $6,500 remaining ($10,800 minus tax of $4,300 at a 40 per cent tax rate).

The Government's share of your RRSP contribution (your tax refund) and the earnings on this amount are equal to and, in effect, pay the taxes on the total amount accumulated in the RRSP.

RRSPS ELIMINATE TAX ON YOUR NET INVESTMENT

Total RRSP Contribution (10% Compounded Annually)

Year	Net Investment		Tax Refund Contributed		Total in RRSP
1	$ 600	+	$ 400	=	$ 1,000
25	$6,500	+	$4,300	=	$ 10,800
Less: Tax at 40%					(4,300)
Net proceeds					$ 6,500

Compare this with a one-time investment outside the RRSP where you are able to invest only your after-tax amount (net investment) of $600.

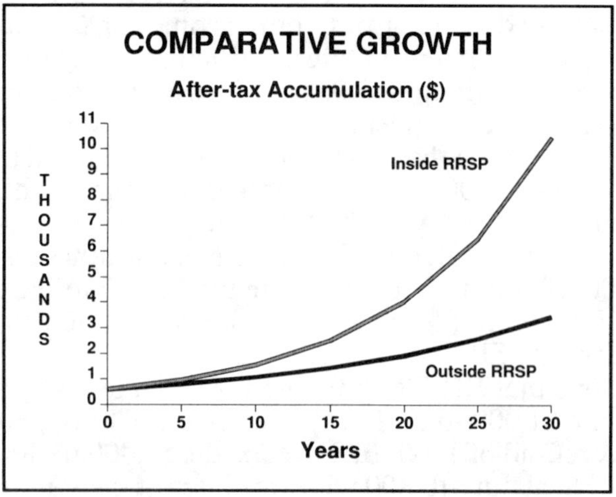

This investment also earns interest at 10 per cent compounded annually, but is subject to tax each year. Therefore, interest is earned at the net rate of 6 per cent annually (10 per cent minus tax at the rate of 40 per cent). After 25 years, you will accumulate only about $2,600 outside the RRSP, which is $3,900 less than is earned on the same amount of net investment in the RRSP.

The longer the funds remain in the RRSP, the better off you will be investing in an RRSP than investing outside an RRSP.

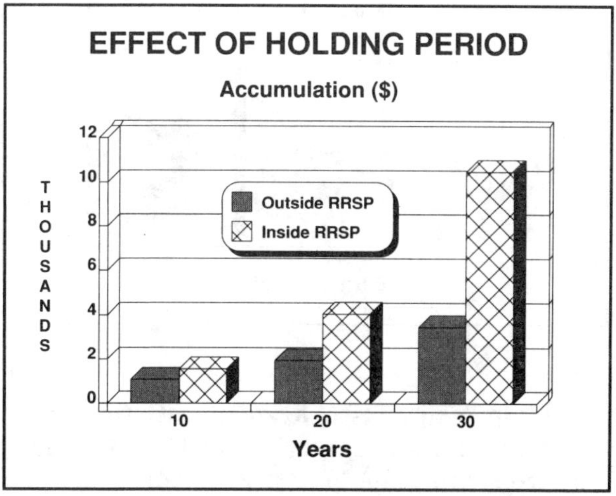

The chart above shows the after-tax growth of an investment made either inside or outside an RRSP. It is assumed that:

- Your marginal tax rate is 40 per cent.
- You make an initial $1,000 RRSP contribution. Your net contribution is therefore $600 (after taking into account your tax refund of $400), the same amount you would have to invest outside the RRSP after taxes.
- The investments each earn 10 per cent compounded annually.
- Tax at 40 per cent is paid when the RRSP is collapsed, and annually outside the RRSP.

In addition, the higher the earnings rate, the better off you will be investing in an RRSP than investing outside an RRSP.

Using the same assumptions as in the previous example, the chart below shows the after-tax growth of a 20-year investment made inside and outside an RRSP.

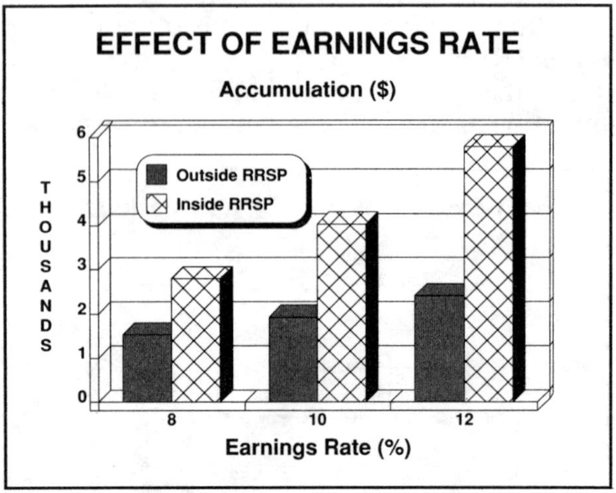

2. RRSPs Help You Stay Ahead of Inflation. Since your investment return is much larger in an RRSP than outside one (because RRSPs eliminate tax on your net investment), you have a much better chance of staying ahead of inflation by using an RRSP to save for your retirement years.

For example, if you can earn 10 per cent annually, your marginal tax rate is 40 per cent and the inflation rate is 5 per cent annually, your after-tax real return on your investment (i.e., after allowing for inflation and taxes) is only 1 per cent (10 per cent minus taxes at the rate of 40 per cent on 10 per cent, minus inflation of 5 per cent). Compare this with using an RRSP. Since the RRSP eliminates tax on your net investment, the only factor to take into consideration when determining your real return is inflation. Thus, if you can earn 10 per cent, your real return with the RRSP is 5 per cent annually (10 per cent minus inflation of 5 per cent).

The chart below compares net investments of $1,000 inside and outside an RRSP after allowing for the effects of inflation at 5 per cent and for tax at 40 per cent on funds withdrawn from the RRSP. Income earned outside the RRSP is taxed at 40 per cent annually. The investments each earn 10 per cent compounded annually.

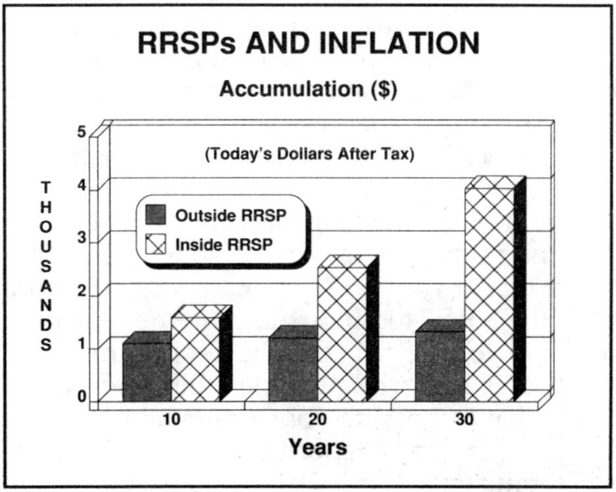

The chart below examines the effect that inflation, at the rates of 4 per cent and 6 per cent per year, has on $1,000 over various periods.

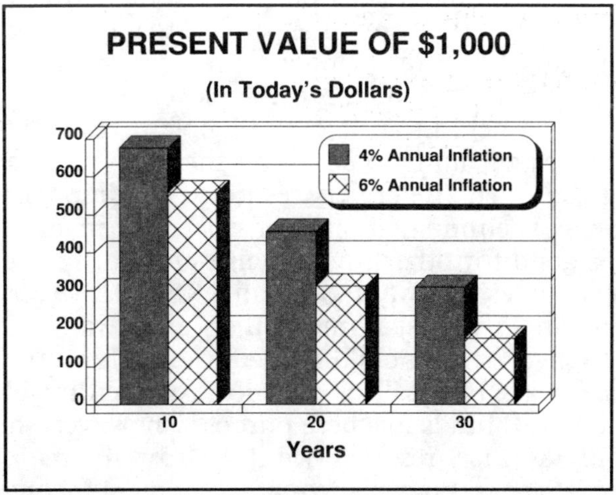

For example, if the inflation rate averages 6 per cent, $1,000 today will be worth about $560 in ten years expressed in terms of today's dollars. In other words, today's $1,000 will lose about 44 per cent of its purchasing power if inflation averages 6 per cent for the next ten years.

3. RRSPs Can Be the Best Way to Save for Your Retirement Years. Because RRSPs eliminate tax on your net investment and they are so effective at combatting inflation, it is likely that an RRSP will be the best way you can save for your retirement, especially if you do not participate in an employer-sponsored pension plan.

The earlier in your working life you begin contributing to an RRSP, the more you maximize your contribution each year, and the earlier you contribute each year, the more will be available in the RRSP to fund your retirement income. Make no mistake! If you fail to contribute or to maximize your contributions as early as possible, the amount of RRSP money available to provide your retirement income will be lessened. You can look forward to a smaller retirement income as a result.

4. RRSPs Are Almost as Flexible as Investing Outside an RRSP. RRSPs are very flexible. You can withdraw funds from an RRSP at any time, assuming the plan's rules permit withdrawals; however, the amount withdrawn must be brought into income for tax purposes in that year. You can "mature" an RRSP at any time (subject to any restrictions in the plan) and begin receiving a retirement income. A wide variety of Canadian (and a specified level of foreign) investments can be held in an RRSP. Eligible investments range from savings accounts to common shares to mortgages (including your own, under very restricted conditions).

Since tax is eliminated on your net RRSP investment, an RRSP is good for other investment purposes. For instance, younger couples may want to use an RRSP to save for a down payment on their first home. Others may want to use an RRSP to save for their children's education, for future emergencies, for a sabbatical, or even for extended travel. Withdrawing RRSP funds for these purposes, however, should be done only as a last resort, since it destroys the main RRSP function of generating an adequate retirement income. Once you withdraw funds from an RRSP, you cannot replace the amount withdrawn. You can make only your normal annual contributions. If you do decide to use an RRSP to save for a non-retirement purpose, it is still best to maximize contributions.

CONTRIBUTION RULES AND RRSP MECHANICS

You may have any number of RRSP contracts at the same time with any number of different financial entities (issuers).

Your contributions may be made each year and are deductible from income for tax purposes, within specific limits, in the year they are made. Contributions made in the first 60 days of the year are deductible in that year or in the immediately preceding year. Starting in 1991, unused deduction room may be carried forward for use in future years. Any income or capital gain arising in the RRSP is not immediately subject to tax, provided certain requirements are met. However, capital gains and dividends lose their special tax status when earned within an RRSP, and are fully taxed when withdrawn. Capital gains and dividends may therefore best be earned outside the RRSP. Tax is payable only when you withdraw funds or begin to receive a retirement income from the RRSP.

Who Can Contribute?

Anyone with earned income, as defined below, may contribute to an RRSP. However, since you must arrange to receive a retirement income from your RRSP by December 31 of the year you turn 71, no further contributions can be made past this date. If you are 71 or older, you can still contribute to a spousal RRSP if your spouse is under 71. If you have not yet reached 71, but you are receiving an RRSP retirement income, you may continue to contribute to your own RRSP.

Children under the age of 18 may contribute to an RRSP, assuming theyhave "earned income" and meet all the relevant RRSP rules. However, you may have trouble finding an issuer willing to enter into an RRSP contract with a minor. Some taxpayers have made contributions (for which no deduction is received) to their child's RRSP in order to split income with the child and reduce the family's overall tax bill. Depending on how long the funds are left in the RRSP and the child's tax rate at the time the funds are withdrawn, the tax deferral advantage may be sufficient to offset the increased tax cost.

1990 Contribution Rules

Individuals who are not members of pension plans or deferred profit sharing plans (DPSPs) may make a deductible contribution to their RRSP of up to 20 per cent of their earned income in the year to a maximum of $7,500. If you are employed in the year and are a member of a pension plan (other than the CPP or QPP) and are or may become entitled to benefits in respect of the year out of contributions made or to be made by you or by someone else on your behalf (e.g., your employer), or you are a beneficiary of a DPSP to which a contribution was made in the year, you may contribute up to 20 per cent of earned income in that year to a maximum of $3,500, minus all deductible contributions made by you in the year in respect of any RPP contributions. The $3,500 maximum applies whether or not you or your employer made a contribution to the RPP in the year. Individuals cannot gain access to the higher $7,500 RRSP limit by arranging for the termination or suspension of benefits or contributions to pension plans or DPSPs.

Contribution Limits in 1991 and Subsequent Years

Individuals Who Are Not Members of RPPs or DPSPs. Commencing in 1991, the RRSP contribution limit for individuals who are not members of RPPs or DPSPs is 18 per cent of the prior year's earned income to a specific dollar maximum, which is phased in as follows:

1991	$11,500
1992	12,500
1993	13,500
1994	14,500
1995	15,500

For example, the maximum RRSP contribution for 1991 will be 18 per cent of earned income in 1990 to a maximum of $11,500. To put it another way, if you want to contribute the maximum of $11,500 to your RRSP in respect of 1991, you need earned income in 1990 of at least $63,888.89. Starting in 1996, the $15,500 figure will be indexed according to the growth in the "Industrial Aggregate" wage.

Members of DPSPs or Money Purchase RPPs. For members of DPSPs, or money purchase RPPs (those in which accumulated contributions and earnings in the plan are used at retirement to purchase the best possible pension), the RRSP contribution limit is 18 per cent of the previous year's earned income to the dollar maximums for the current year noted above, minus an amount called the "pension adjustment" (PA). The PA for these individuals is simply the total of all employee and employer contributions and re-allocated forfeitures made in the previous calendar year to all money purchase RPPs and DPSPs (employees cannot contribute to DPSPs after 1988). Amounts re-allocated in 1990 that relate to pre-1990 forfeitures are not included in the 1990 money purchase or DPSP PA.

For example, assume that in 1990 your employer contributes $1,800 to your money purchase RPP and you contribute $1,600 to the plan. Your earned income in 1990 is $48,000 so your maximum RRSP contribution for 1991 is $8,640 (the lesser of $11,500 and 18 per cent of $48,000). From this you must deduct your PA from the previous year (1990) of $3,400 (RPP contributions of $1,800 and $1,600). Thus, your allowable RRSP contribution in 1991 is $5,240 ($8,640 minus $3,400).

Members of Defined Benefit RPPs. For these individuals (who are guaranteed a specific pension by their RPP), the RRSP contribution limit is 18 per cent of the previous year's earned income to the dollar maximum for the current year, as noted above, minus a PA that reflects the value of accrued benefits under the RPP in respect of the previous year. (If the individual is also a member of a DPSP, the PA will also reflect the amount of the employer's contribution.)

To illustrate the PA mechanism in very basic terms, assume that your earned income is $40,000 and your defined benefit RPP provides half the allowable maximum benefits. Thus, your maximum eligible RRSP contribution is $7,200 (18 per cent of $40,000) minus the PA. Since maximum benefits under a defined benefit RPP are the same in dollar terms as the maximum RRSP contribution allowed, the PA is one-half of $7,200 = $3,600 minus $1,000 = $2,600. Thus, you are allowed to contribute up to $4,600 to the RRSP ($7,200 minus $2,600). The $1,000 is an ad hoc amount that allows for differences in ancillary benefits among defined benefit RPPs.

Pension Adjustment for a Year

The PA, which will apply to reduce RRSP contributions for 1991 and subsequent years, is a new concept designed to ensure that pension plan (or DPSP) members in different plans, with similar incomes, but different benefit rates, will have equal access to tax assistance to help build their retirement income. A PA essentially represents the portion of the total RRSP deduction limit used up by virtue of the retirement benefits that accumulate to an individual's credit in RPPs or DPSPs. The PA for a calendar year is used to determine the RRSP deduction limit for the following year.

For example, a member of a pension plan that provides generous benefits will have a relatively high PA, which will lessen the individual's ability to contribute to an RRSP. Many members of non-contributory defined benefit plans could find their ability to contribute to an RRSP restricted to $1,000 annually, starting in 1991. Less generous pension plans will result in a smaller PA and larger allowable RRSP contributions.

The Size of the PA. Calculating the PA can be either very easy or very difficult, depending on the situation. An individual whose retirement income is funded solely through RRSPs will have no PA, and the RRSP deduction limit will be 18 per cent of earned income in the previous year, to the RRSP dollar maximums for the current year noted in the table above. The PA of a member of a DPSP will equal the total employer contributions to the plan and allocations made to the member in respect of the previous year. The PA of a member of a money purchase RPP will be the total of the employee's and employer's contributions to the plan, plus amounts allocated to the member, in the previous year. Determining the PA for a member of a defined benefit RPP is much more complex. For defined benefit provisions, the PA is calculated by applying a formula designed to equate the value of benefits accrued under the plan in the year to the equivalent of the contribution that would have been required to fund the benefits under a money purchase arrangement such as an RRSP.

Employers are required to calculate PAs for each employee, starting in 1990. They will report their first PAs (relating to 1990) as part of the T4 reporting process required by February 28, 1991. Once employees receive their 1990 T4, they will be able to determine precisely their 1991 RRSP contribution limit. Revenue Canada will then advise all taxpayers of their 1991 RRSP deduction limit late in 1991. Similar procedures will be followed in subsequent years.

Members of defined benefit pension plans, for whom the PA calculation is most difficult, can take some heart from the fact that their employer and Revenue Canada will have the burden of doing the calculation. Most people would be in a position to make their RRSP contribution for the current year on the basis of the T4 reporting. However, it may be prudent to wait until late in the year, when Revenue Canada sends out official notification of the permissible RRSP deduction limits for the year.

Past Service Pension Adjustment. Like the PA, the past service pension adjustment (PSPA) decreases the RRSP deduction limit. A PSPA represents the reduction in an individual's RRSP contribution limit associated with new or additional benefits provided to him or her under a defined benefit provision of an RPP in respect of service before the current calendar year. Employers with defined benefit RPPs must have a PSPA certified by Revenue Canada if additional retirement benefits in respect of post-1989 service are provided retroactively.

Earned Income

Your RRSP contribution limit is based on a percentage of your earned income while you are resident in Canada, which will include the following:

- salary or wages before the deduction of RPP contributions and unemployment insurance premiums;
- income from royalties in respect of a work or invention of which the taxpayer was the author or inventor;
- income from carrying on a business, either alone or as a partner actively engaged in the business;
- net rental income, whether active or passive, from real property;
- payments from supplementary unemployment benefit plans;
- alimony or maintenance included in income for tax purposes, including that received by a common-law spouse;
- net research grants;

less the following:

- losses from carrying on business either alone or as a partner actively engaged in the business;
- net rental losses from real property;
- deductible alimony or maintenance payments.

Seven-Year Carryforward Rule

Commencing in 1991, if an individual contributes less than the maximum allowable amount to an RRSP in any particular year, this "unused RRSP deduction room" may be made up by contributions of more than the maximums otherwise permitted in later years. The full amount of a prior year's unused deduction room can be used without limitation at any time during the seven years after it arises. After seven years, certain restrictions may apply, but the amount that can be contributed in respect of unused RRSP deduction room will not be reduced below 3.5 times the RRSP dollar limit for the particular year.

Waiting until later years to make up deduction room carried forward may result in a tax cost and in many cases will result in a smaller accumulation in the RRSP by the time you retire. There also appears to be little point in delaying your contribution to a later year when you expect your tax rate will be higher, as your tax saving may be offset by the cost of giving up the tax shelter advantage that would have resulted from earlier contributions.

Under the fully mature system, the annual RRSP deduction limit that Revenue Canada will report to individuals before the end of the taxation year will be equal to:

- balance of unused RRSP deduction room carried forward from the previous year;
- plus 18 per cent of earned income (up to the dollar maximum for the year) less all pension adjustments (PAs) calculated by employers, both determined with reference to earnings in the immediately preceding taxation year;
- less any net Past Service Pension Adjustment (calculated by employers who sponsor a defined benefit pension plan and make retroactive upgrades to it) reported and certified during the taxation year.

Withdrawals from an RRSP

RRSPs are intended to be held until retirement, at which point you would arrange an RRSP retirement income. However, there are no government restrictions against withdrawing funds from most RRSPs at any time. The amount withdrawn is included in income for tax purposes. If the withdrawal relates to a non-deductible excess RRSP contribution, an offsetting deduction may be available. Check to see that your RRSP itself does not restrict withdrawals.

Under a rule that became effective in 1986, you may withdraw any amount from your RRSP, if the plan so allows. Pre-1986 RRSPs will have to be amended by the issuer to allow such a partial withdrawal. Before 1986, any withdrawal caused immediate deregistration; the entire plan had to be collapsed in order to receive the funds. Generally, the plan issuer would require you to give notice that you intend to withdraw funds from the plan. Some plans require that you give up to one or two months' notice for withdrawal. The issuer of the RRSP is required to withhold tax at the following rates on any RRSP amount paid to you.

Amount	Canadian Residents Except Residents of Quebec (%)	Quebec Residents (%)
$5,000 or less	10	18
$5,001 to $15,000	20	30
Over $15,000	30	35

At one time, you could transfer the amount that you wanted to bring into income from your RRSP to a registered retirement income fund (RRIF - a plan under which you receive retirement income) and immediately withdraw the amount from the RRIF without any tax being withheld. Now, however, withholding is required on the portion of any RRIF payment in excess of the minimum annual amount required to be paid from a RRIF.

If you are withdrawing relatively large amounts from an RRSP or an RRIF, you should consider making several separate withdrawals to lessen the withholding rate and perhaps making withdrawals over several years to avoid a high marginal rate of tax on a portion of the funds.

Spousal RRSPs

Any amount of your regular RRSP contribution can be contributed, in whole or in part, to an RRSP of which your spouse is the annuitant, whether or not your spouse makes an RRSP contribution in his or her own right (special rollover contributions cannot be made to a spousal plan). You should make the contribution directly to the trustee of the plan and have it receipted to you so that you can prove that you made the payment.

Spousal RRSP contributions are extremely valuable for splitting income on retirement. For example, assume that your spouse will have few or no other sources of pension income, besides those from the government. If your spouse's marginal tax rate will be 25 per cent on retirement while yours will be 45 per cent, you and your spouse will have up to an extra 20 cents on every dollar of RRSP retirement income available. Expressed in percentage terms, your after-tax disposable income on the RRSP amounts after retiring could increase by more than 36 per cent. In addition, your spouse will have income eligible for the tax credit on pension income when he or she reaches age 65.

Contributions to a spousal RRSP reduce the amount that you can otherwise contribute to your own RRSP. In other words, the total of amounts contributed by you to both plans is limited by your total deduction room available. You may not transfer amounts from your own RRSPs, RPPs or deferred profit sharing plans (DPSPs) to a spousal RRSP, except on marriage breakdown or death.

If you are 71 years of age or older and have deduction room available, you may still make contributions to your spouse's RRSP if he or she has not reached age 71.

Within 60 days of the date of death, it is possible for the legal representative of an estate to make a contribution to a spousal RRSP where the spouse is under 71. This permits a deduction of such an amount on the deceased's final return of income.

Withdrawals from a Spousal RRSP. A special rule prevents married couples from using a spousal RRSP to split income and hence reduce taxes. If your spouse receives funds from any of his or her RRSPs to which you have made a spousal contribution, from any commuted annuity from such a plan, or from any registered retirement income fund (RRIF) that receives funds from such a plan in excess of the minimum amount required to be paid from the RRIF, then an amount equal to the lesser of:

(a) the amount received by your spouse; or

(b) the aggregate of contributions made by you to any plans on behalf of your spouse that were paid by you in the year of receipt of the funds and the two immediately preceding years (not including amounts previously added back to your income);

is added to your income and taxed in your hands. The excess, if any, of (a) over (b) is included in your spouse's income.

The following example will help explain this rule. The following amounts are contributed to your spouse's RRSP:

Year	Amounts Contributed By You	By Spouse
1	$2,000	–
2	–	$4,000
3	$1,000	–

If your spouse removes $4,000 from the RRSP at the end of Year 3, $3,000 is included in your income and $1,000 in your spouse's income. If your spouse had contributed the $4,000 to a separate plan in Year 2 and then withdrawn the $4,000 in Year 3, the entire amount would be included in your spouse's income, assuming you had not made a contribution to that particular plan.

This restriction on withdrawal is applicable despite the number of different RRSPs, annuities or RRIFs the spouse may have or whether funds have been transferred from a "spousal" RRSP to another RRSP to which no spousal contributions have been made directly.

If your spouse receives funds from an RRSP to which only he or she contributed, or includes in income the value of a commuted annuity or a payment from an RRIF in excess of the minimum amount, and the annuity or RRIF was acquired from an RRSP to which only your spouse contributed, the amounts do not have to be included in your income, even though you have made spousal RRSP contributions to other plans in the current year or the immediately preceding two years.

The rule will also apply to the tax-free transfer you can make to a spousal RRSP of up to $6,000 of periodic payments you might receive from a registered pension plan or deferred profit sharing plan. This tax-free transfer started in 1989 and ends in 1994.

The rule will not apply on your death or if you are divorced or separated and living apart from your spouse. It also does not apply if your spouse makes certain tax-free transfers of funds, such as from an RRIF to an RRSP annuity.

Locked-In RRSPs

Pension reform requires the use of locked-in RRSPs to facilitate the portability of pension benefits. Upon termination of employment, employees should have the option of leaving their pension entitlements with their former employer, transferring them to a pension plan with their new employer, if the new employer is agreeable, or transferring them to a locked-in RRSP, which would be more restrictive than an ordinary RRSP and would not provide for withdrawals prior to retirement. Typically, a locked-in RRSP will provide that upon your retirement, you will have to use the RRSP funds to purchase an annuity. Certain provincial pension laws already require this treatment on transfers from RPPs to RRSPs.

Types of Contributions

You may contribute either cash or property to an RRSP depending on the type of RRSP you have. The value of your contribution of property is the fair market value of the property at the time of contribution. You are deemed to have disposed of the property at fair market value when it is transferred to the RRSP and a gain or loss may result. Any gain must be included in income for tax purposes, although capital gains will be eligible for your lifetime capital gains exemption. Any loss, however, is denied to you and cannot be used to offset gains. Do not, therefore, sell "losers" to your RRSP. If you contribute a non-qualified investment (see below), the fair market value of that investment is included in computing your income for the year of contribution.

Borrowing for Your RRSP Contribution

Any interest paid on funds borrowed to make an RRSP contribution after November 12, 1981, is not deductible for tax purposes. Interest on loans for RRSP contributions before that date continues to be deductible. For current contributions, you are likely better off borrowing to enable you to make a contribution than not contributing at all. This certainly would be the case if a portion of your deduction room were about to expire. It also may make sense to borrow now to make a contribution rather than waiting several years to contribute in respect of unused deduction room carried forward, because you can begin sheltering income from tax in the RRSP much sooner than you otherwise would.

Transfers to and from an RRSP

The new system is designed with a great deal of flexibility. Within the limits, contributions may be made for an individual in any registered plan or combination of plans. With the requirement for portable pensions by pension benefit legislation, an increasing amount of registered monies will be transferred from plan to plan, or end up in individual RRSPs. Group RRSPs, with their administrative simplicity, are likely to become more popular.

Direct transfers of lump sum amounts are generally allowed between plans on a tax-free basis, subject to a prescribed maximum. But, after 1988, individuals are no longer able to withdraw amounts from one plan during the year and subsequently contribute such amounts to an RRSP within 60 days after the end of the year. Tax-deferred transfers must be made directly from one plan to another. After 1989, RRSP amounts can be transferred only before the maturity of the plan.

Certain transfers will not be permitted. For example, a plan member's share of an actuarial surplus under a defined benefit provision received after March 27, 1988, will not be transferable to another plan. In addition, after 1988, amounts forfeited by terminating employees in money purchase pension plans and deferred profit sharing plans will have to be returned to the employer or re-allocated to other employees.

The ability to roll over pension and RRSP annuity payments into an RRSP on a tax-deferred basis is discontinued after 1989. As a transitional measure, periodic RPP or DPSP payments will be transferable to a spousal RRSP from 1989 to 1994 up to a $6,000 annual limit.

The tax-free rollover of a retiring allowance into an RRSP is still allowed. For service years after 1988, the limit is $2,000 per year of service. Up to and including 1988, this may be increased by $1,500 for each year for which no employer contributions to an RPP or DPSP are vested. To avoid tax being withheld on the retiring allowance, the employer can make the transfer directly to the RRSP.

Accumulated amounts in RRSPs may be transferred on a tax-free basis to another RRSP, to an RRIF, or to an RPP. The amounts must be transferred directly by the issuer of the RRSP. If you receive the amount directly, it must be included in your income for tax purposes and the tax-free transfer then cannot be made. After 1989, such transfers to your own RRSP, RRIF, or RPP can be made only before the plan matures.

A transfer from your RRSP to an RPP could prove beneficial if your employer is also contributing to the RPP. For example, your defined benefit plan may have been upgraded to provide better benefits, but you are required to finance half of the necessary funding along with your employer. Assuming your participation in the upgrade is voluntary, you would compare your potential RRSP retirement income that could be generated from the amount of funding required by the RPP, with the upgraded RPP benefits, to determine if it would be worthwhile transferring the amount from your RRSP.

You are allowed to make direct transfers of commuted annuity amounts and payments from an RRIF in excess of the required minimum payment, to an RRSP, another RRIF, or you may acquire any of the RRSP-type annuities. The annuity must provide for equal annual or more frequent payments, starting not later than one year after the transfer.

A "refund of premiums" (a defined term for RRSP purposes) received by a spouse or dependent person from the RRSP of a deceased person can also be transferred on a tax-free basis to your RRSP. The tax-free transfer of RRSP amounts to your spouse on marriage breakdown is also possible.

RRSPs and the Minimum Tax

Some taxpayers are required to recalculate taxable income for purposes of the minimum tax to ensure a certain level of tax is paid despite the number and amount of deductions from income they otherwise might have. One of the items not allowed as a deduction for determining income for alternative minimum tax purposes is an RPP or RRSP contribution, whether made in respect of the current year or deduction room carried forward. (Essentially, only lump sum transfers from a DPSP or a pension plan, or direct transfers from one RRSP to another, are permitted RPP or RRSP deductions for purposes of the minimum tax.)

Two very general observations can be made. First, only upper income Canadians are affected because those with income below $40,000 are not subject to the tax. Second, because of the potential for large deductions from income, those persons making contributions in respect of unused deduction room carried forward from several years are more likely to be affected than those simply making their annual contribution.

Amounts for which a deduction from income is not effective because the minimum tax is applicable may be effectively carried forward to the immediately following seven years. This occurs because the difference between tax normally payable and the minimum tax payable is allowed as a deduction from tax payable in the following years, but only to the extent your regular tax liability in that year exceeds your minimum tax liability.

Penalties, Special Taxes, and Deregistration

Excess Contributions. Annual pre-1991 contributions made in excess of the greater of $5,500 or the actual amount deductible for tax purposes are subject to a tax of 1 per cent a month on this excess until the amount is withdrawn. The $5,500 annual threshold below which there is no penalty is eliminated for contributions after 1990, and any "cumulative excess amount" over a lifetime threshold of $8,000 will be subject to the 1 per cent penalty. Such an excess amount can be withdrawn tax-free in the year an assessment notice is received in respect of the year in which the excess contribution was made or in the immediately following year. If the excess contribution is not withdrawn, it is, in effect, subject to double taxation since no deduction for the contribution is allowed and it is taxed when eventually received as retirement income.

Foreign Investments. Generally you are allowed to invest 12 per cent (in 1990) of the cost of your RRSP investments in qualified foreign securities. (The percentage is to increase by two percentage points annually, reaching 20 per cent for 1994 and subsequent taxation years.) If you exceed this level, your RRSP is subject to tax at the rate of 1 per cent a month on the excess amount invested in foreign securities for each month the excess remains in the RRSP. You may exceed the 10 per cent limit, within certain limits, if you make investments in eligible small businesses.

Non-qualified Investments. If your RRSP acquires an investment that is not a qualified RRSP investment, the fair market value of the investment at the time of acquisition is included in your income in that year. In the year the RRSP disposes of the investment, you may deduct from your income the lesser of the proceeds of disposition and the amount previously added to income. In that year, under the current rules, the amount you are eligible to deduct for your contribution to an RRSP based on your earned income is reduced by the amount deducted from income in respect of the non-qualified investment. As well, tax is payable at the top marginal rate by the RRSP on the income earned by the non-qualified investment.

If a qualified investment in your RRSP becomes a non-qualified investment, the RRSP must pay a special tax equal to 1 per cent of the fair market value of the investment at the time of acquisition for each month the investment retains its non-qualified status, or until the investment is disposed of by the RRSP, assuming the value of the investment was not included in your income.

Stock Option Agreements. If an RRSP enters into a stock option agreement, other than acquiring options listed on a stock exchange, the RRSP may be subject to tax at the rate of 1 per cent a month on the price the RRSP has agreed to pay for the stock beginning in the month the RRSP enters into the agreement.

Borrowing Money or Carrying on Business. If your RRSP borrows money at any point in the year, tax is payable by the RRSP on all its income each year until the borrowed funds are repaid. An RRSP is a trust and therefore is subject to tax at the maximum personal rate in your province of residence. If the RRSP carries on a business at any time during the year, the resulting business income is subject to tax at regular trust rates.

RRSP as Collateral for a Loan. If any of your RRSP property is used as collateral for a loan, the fair market value of the property used as collateral is added to your income in that particular year. When the RRSP property ceases to be used as collateral, an amount equal to the amount previously added to income less any losses suffered on the loan transaction may be deducted from income. If, however, the RRSP is a depositary-type plan, it will be subject to deregistration should any of the RRSP be pledged, assigned, etc., in which case the entire amount in the plan is included in your income for tax purposes and there is no way that the plan can be subsequently reinstated.

RRSP Buying and Selling Property at Other Than Fair Market Value. If your RRSP acquires property at greater than fair market value or sells property at less than fair market value, the difference between fair market value and the amount paid or received is added to your income in the year the transaction takes place.

Deregistration. RRSPs can be deregistered for a variety of reasons, in which case the fair market value of all the assets of the particular plan are included in income for tax purposes in the year the plan is deregistered. However, issuers will structure your RRSP so as to prevent it from being deregistered in most circumstances (i.e., the contract or arrangement you have with the issuer will prohibit actions that would result in deregistration).

An RRSP will be denied registration or will have its registration revoked if any advantage that is conditional upon the existence of the plan (with certain exceptions) is extended to the annuitant of the plan or to any person with whom he or she is not dealing at arm's length. This provision covers a wide variety of situations, from accepting a "free gift" for opening an RRSP to arranging for your self-directed RRSP to hold your neighbour's low-interest mortgage while your neighbour reciprocates. It does not apply, however, to "bonus" rates of interest on RRSP deposits.

An RRSP will automatically be deregistered if you do not arrange a retirement income to be paid by December 31 of the year you turn 71. The plan is effectively deregistered on the first day of the following year and its full value included in income therefore in the year you turn 72. Some plans provide for an automatic annuity purchase if no other retirement income is arranged, but an annuity may not suit your retirement income needs.

RRSP INVESTMENTS

The more your RRSP investments earn, the better off you will be once you retire. The message may seem trite, but surprisingly few people realize how important it is to maximize returns in an RRSP over the long term. A difference of only two percentage points can make a significant difference in the size of your retirement income.

A higher earnings rate also improves your real return on your RRSP investments, that is, your return after allowing for inflation. For example, if inflation averages 6 per cent, your real return on an RRSP earning 8 per cent annually is about 2 per cent. However, your real return on an RRSP earning 10 per cent annually is about 4 per cent, double the real return on the 8 per cent RRSP.

The chart below compares retirement incomes in today's dollars, that is, after allowing for the effects of inflation in future years at 6 per cent, available from an RRSP if earnings range from 8 per cent to 14 per cent. A 25-year level payment annuity earning 10 per cent compounded annually is assumed to be paid from the RRSP to which $5,000 is contributed annually at the beginning of each year for 25 years.

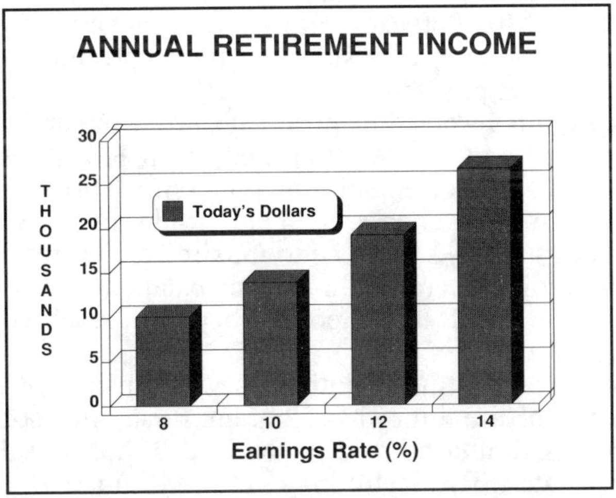

Bear in mind that when comparing yields on various investments, there can be substantial differences between monthly, quarterly, semi-annual and annual compounding over the long term. The shorter the compounding term, the higher the yield. Remember too that the higher the yield, the greater the risk. Stable financial institutions can attract investment dollars more easily than institutions whose track record is less attractive.

Interest, Dividends, or Capital Gains in Your RRSP

Deciding whether your RRSP should hold securities that produce interest, dividends, or capital gains depends on how the investments are taxed outside an RRSP and whether your investment portfolio consists entirely of investments in RRSPs or you also hold investments outside RRSPs. The decision also depends on how well you tolerate risk.

Interest received directly by an individual is taxed at full rates. Canadian dividends are taxed at a lower effective rate because of the dividend tax credit. If you are in the 29 per cent federal tax bracket, dividends are taxed at about two-thirds the rate on interest. In the 17 per cent tax bracket, there could be less than 10 per cent tax on dividends. Capital gains are taxed at three-fourths the rate on interest, but you are entitled to a lifetime $100,000 exemption on capital gains ($500,000 for qualifying shares of a small business corporation or for qualifying farm property).

All amounts received from RRSPs are taxed at full rates. Capital gains and dividends earned in an RRSP lose their identity and are not eligible for preferential tax treatment.

If all your investments are held inside an RRSP, your investment strategy should be to maximize your return over the long term. Generally, this means balancing your investments in the RRSP to the point where you reach your risk tolerance level.

If you have investments both inside and outside RRSPs, the rules of thumb are somewhat different. First, interest-bearing investments should be held in the RRSP, not outside. The reason is that the RRSP eliminates tax on your net investment (the after-tax amount that could be invested outside the

RRSP), whereas interest income is taxed at full rates outside your RRSP. The gross yield on interest-bearing investments inside an RRSP is greater than outside (remember the gross yield on your net RRSP investment is tax-free) and the yield on such investments bears a higher rate of tax if earned outside the RRSP.

Second, since RRSPs effectively eliminate tax on your net investment, preferred shares or common shares that pay dividends should generally be held inside an RRSP, but not if you are then forced to hold interest-bearing securities outside the RRSP. The market tends to equate after-tax rates on investments of similar risk for individuals in the top tax bracket. Thus, if interest is payable at 10 per cent producing an after-tax yield of 5.4 per cent for an individual in the top tax bracket, dividends on preferred shares would be payable at about 7.9 per cent to produce a similar after-tax yield outside the RRSP. However,since RRSPs defer tax, the 10 per cent yield on the interest-bearing security is clearly superior to the dividend yield of 7.9 per cent inside the RRSP.

Third, with the introduction of the lifetime capital gains exemption, there may be little point in holding investments that produce primarily capital gains in an RRSP to the extent any gains are exempt from tax, although RRSPs also eliminate tax on your net investment. This is not to say that you should reduce your RRSP contributions in order to realize capital gains outside your RRSP. Eventually, you may exhaust your capital gains exemption, or want to convert these capital properties to less risky but taxable investments. If you do use your RRSP to hold investments for capital gains, bear in mind that the RRSP should first hold interest-bearing securities and then hold dividend-producing investments.

One other observation is possible concerning the balance of your RRSP investment portfolio. Generally, the younger you are, the more heavily you may want to weight your portfolio in favour of equities. Since you are investing for the long term, you can take advantage of the expected higher return over this period and you are able to weather the ups and downs of the stock market. However, the closer you are to retirement, the more heavily your RRSP (and non-RRSP investments as well) should be weighted toward less risky investments such as interest-bearing securities in order to protect your accumulated capital. At some point, you may want to lock the majority of your funds into investments with guaranteed interest rates so that you can plan the size of your retirement income with some certainty.

Canada Deposit Insurance

Because large sums of money can accumulate in an RRSP, many taxpayers are concerned about protection of RRSP funds, especially in light of the fact that financial institutions can fail. The Canada Deposit Insurance Corporation (CDIC) might cover your RRSP investments, depending on the amount and type of investments held in the RRSP and the financial institution holding the investment.

All chartered banks and federally incorporated trust companies and mortgage loan companies are members of the CDIC. Provincial mortgage loan companies and trust companies may also apply for membership. You should ascertain if your RRSP issuer has such coverage.

While an RRSP trust itself is not insured, the investments held by the RRSP that qualify for deposit insurance are insured, as are investments registered as RRSPs (depositary RRSPs). Qualifying investments include savings and chequing accounts, and guaranteed investment certificates and term deposits that are redeemable within five years. The insurance does not apply to foreign currency deposits, such as U.S. dollar savings accounts or U.S. dollar GICs.

The maximum insurance coverage is $60,000 per customer per member institution. If you have RRSPs with more than one member institution, whether directly or through a self-directed plan, your coverage ismultiplied. Similarly, if you have a self-directed RRSP that holds investments from various member financial institutions, each of these investments will be covered separately. CDIC insurance on your RRSP is separate from CDIC insurance on investments you hold personally, which in effect doubles your maximum coverage at one institution to $120,000.

In some provinces, certain non-member institutions, such as credit unions, have their own insurance plans that may cover RRSP investments. RRSPs issued by insurance companies are not covered by the CDIC.

Types of RRSPs

RRSP investment vehicles are available in the following major categories:

- insurance-type, where you contract to pay a certain amount, usually periodically, in return for a retirement income of a certain size paid periodically;
- depositary RRSPs, where your deposits are made directly with the issuer; and
- RRSP trusts, the most common being self-directed RRSPs where you make the investment decisions.

Insurance Company RRSPs

Insurance companies now sell RRSPs that are similar to and competitive with RRSPs sold by other financial institutions. Most insurance companies offer daily interest or variable rate RRSPs and guaranteed rate RRSPs with varying terms.

These RRSPs are usually defined as life insurance and are structured as annuities, but there is generally no life or mortality element attached. The life insurance companies generally guarantee to convert the RRSPs to annuities upon retirement at the higher of a stated minimum rate or the current market rate. However, whether you annuitize these funds is strictly your decision. Your RRSP has a cash value and can be transferred to another issuer at any time.

The most significant feature of life insurance RRSPs not available elsewhere is that, because of the way they are structured, they are, in many cases, protected from creditors if the annuitant goes bankrupt. However, life insurance RRSPs are usually not protected under the Canada Deposit Insurance Corporation, although they are self-insured by the insurance industry.

Many insurance companies also offer fixed income and equity segregated fund RRSPs, which are similar to mutual fund RRSPs.

RRSPs Sold by Issuing Financial Institutions

Savings Account and Guaranteed RRSPs. Most financial institutions, including banks, trust companies, credit unions, caisses populaires, and insurance companies, and securities dealers and brokers offer a variety of savings account and guaranteed RRSPs.

Savings account or variable rate RRSPs are the least risky of all RRSP investments. In most instances, they are simply daily interest savings accounts, or they may be invested in short-term guaranteed securities. There are usually no start-up fees, as little as $100 can be invested, and withdrawal fees are nominal.

Savings account RRSPs are popular because of their flexibility. They are available almost everywhere, can be opened and closed with little fuss, and funds can be transferred easily to other RRSPs with little notice and usually no fees. In times of rising interest rates, they can be more attractive than guaranteed rate interest-bearing RRSPs because the rate of return follows the rise in rates. The opposite is true, however, when interest rates are falling. Savings account RRSPs also can be used by persons contributing to their RRSPs at the last minute. Their funds earn a modest amount of income while they take the next few months to evaluate the myriad of RRSP investments with no pressure and make the choice that suits them best. Some savings accounts pay a higher rate of interest if a minimum amount, usually $5,000 to $10,000, is kept on deposit.

Guaranteed RRSPs encompass a broad range of investment vehicles. The feature common to all is that the interest rate on the security is locked in for a specific period of time, ranging anywhere from one to five years, and with some securities, over 20 years. The most common types are guaranteed investment certificates (GICs) and term deposits. You must hold GICs to maturity; term deposits can generally be cashed at any time, but with a penalty.

The terms of these RRSP investments vary among issuers. The interest on some compounds annually and on others semi-annually or even monthly. On some, the interest is reinvested at the stated rate on the security, while on others it may be reinvested in a savings account at a much lower rate.

Several financial institutions offer longer-term guaranteed RRSP investments, some over 20 years, through strips (see below). These and other guaranteed securities, such as treasury bills, Canada Savings Bonds and other government or corporate debt instruments, generally can be held only through a self-directed RRSP.

Strips. Strips are one of the more attractive RRSP investments. These are the periodic (usually semi-annual) interest coupons stripped from high-quality, long-term, government-issued or -backed guaranteed bonds. Each of the coupons and the residual bond itself are sold separately. Because each of the coupons on a particular bond has a different future date when the interest amount becomes payable, the coupons are sold at a discount that provides for a specific yield based on current interest rates and the time remaining to maturity. Strips are flexible in that short- or long-term maturities of practically any duration are available. Strips are usually purchased through a self-directed RRSP.

Investment Funds. A number of investment funds (often called mutual funds) qualify as investments for RRSPs. One of their main advantages is that, for a nominal fee, you have professionals managing your RRSP funds. In theory, a professional should do much better over the long term than an average investor. The three main types are fixed income funds (including bond funds, guaranteed income funds, and money market funds), equity funds, and other specialty funds such as real estate or precious metal funds. Not all funds qualify as RRSP investments.

An RRSP contribution is invested in units of the particular fund, which are usually valued daily or weekly based on the current fair market value of the fund's assets. All earnings of the fund for RRSP purposes, less expenses, are automatically reinvested in units of the fund at the current fair market value on a periodic basis. A number of funds charge a fee upon purchase (a front-end load). All funds are professionally managed and an annual management fee is levied against the fund's assets.

Any RRSP, including an investment fund eligible for RRSP investing, cannot, in general terms, have more than 12 per cent (in 1990, increasing by two percentage points annually to reach 20 per cent for 1994 and subsequent taxation years) of the cost of its assets invested in foreign securities, although this percentage can be increased if the RRSP or fund invests in qualifying Canadian small businesses. The fund manager will ensure that the fund continues to be an eligible RRSP investment.

Fixed Income Funds. The term is something of a misnomer. These funds may invest in guaranteed securities, but their daily value is anything but fixed or guaranteed. Investments of these funds include government and corporate bonds, treasury bills, mortgages and even preferred shares. Some funds specialize in particular investments, such as mortgages or short-term securities. Funds investing primarily in bonds or mortgages should be looked on as longer-term investments, while the money market funds, which invest in treasury bills and similar securities, can be held over the short term.

Equity Funds. Equity funds offer the highest potential returns of the conventional RRSP investment vehicles over the long term, but with greater risk. They invest primarily in public company common and preferred shares. Some funds are speculative and some are conservative. The quality of the current management is probably the most important factor to consider when choosing a fund.

Equity funds are not for the short-term investor. Their superior average performance is valid historically only over terms of at least five years. You should consider holding equity funds for a much longer period of time, and you might consider investing in several different funds to spread your risk.

The published long-term earnings records of the numerous investment funds are not necessarily determined in the same manner. Try to uncover the compounding method used in particular funds as well as the way earnings of the fund are treated. The size of front-end loads, and management and administration fees, definitely make a difference in the short run, but generally do not have a large impact over the long haul. You should never forget the fact that everyone selling RRSP investments is in business to make a profit from your contribution.

Specialty Funds. Real estate and precious metal funds have not proved to be overly popular in the last few years. They also should be looked on as highly speculative compared with other RRSP investments and therefore only suitable to a small percentage of investors.

Specialty RRSP Investments. These include U.S. dollar GICs and provincial venture capital programs offering incentives for investments in smaller high-risk companies. In Ontario, for example, these can be structured as public companies that are eligible RRSP investments.

RRSPs are also permitted to invest directly in certain Canadian small businesses as long as the annuitant of the RRSP has no significant connection with the business. To encourage such investments, your RRSP is allowed to invest $3 in foreign securities for every $1 invested in an eligible small business. This allowable foreign investment is in excess of the normal limit.

Investments in shares or debt of a Canadian company that invests primarily in foreign securities (except shares of a class that had no shares issued after December 4, 1985, and the corporation is listed on a prescribed stock exchange) no longer are considered to be Canadian property. Such shares qualify as foreign property for purposes of the 12 per cent limit in 1990 (increasing by two percentage points annually to reach 20 per cent for 1994 and subsequent taxation years).

Self-Directed RRSPs

Self-directed RRSPs generally provide convenient monthly reporting from one source and facilitate the spreading and varying of risk. As investment objectives change over time, the make-up of a self-directed investment portfolio can be updated, providing maximum flexibility.

Self-directed plans are currently offered by brokers, trust companies and several banks. The annual administrative fee varies from $50 to several hundred dollars. If the fee is paid directly to the RRSP issuer and not deducted from your RRSP contribution, it is deductible from income for tax purposes. The trustee holds all securities and arranges for all purchases and sales. One of the advantages of opening a self-directed plan with a full-service broker or dealer is that you gain access to his or her research and advice. Of course, the dealer or broker also handles all transactions and charges the usual commissions.

RRSP issuers generally suggest that self-directed RRSPs contain a minimum of $10,000. It is also usually conceded that an investor should have at least $20,000 available for investing to be reasonably diversified.

Whether a specific investment qualifies for an RRSP is of crucial concern to taxpayers with self-directed plans. The following is a partial listing of the more common qualified RRSP investments:

- money in Canadian currency (but not gold coins such as the Canadian maple leaf coin);
- GICs (can generally be issued in any currency);
- term deposits;
- bonds, debentures, notes, mortgages, hypothecs or similar obligations issued by a Canadian government (federal, provincial, or municipal) or guaranteed by the federal government, including Canada Savings Bonds;
- bonds, debentures, etc. of corporations whose shares are listed on a Canadian stock exchange;
- shares listed on a Canadian stock exchange;
- shares listed on certain foreign stock exchanges;
- most listed warrants, rights, etc., provided they contain the right to acquire eligible investments;
- units or shares of investment funds or insurance company pooled funds;
- annuities issued by a Canadian financial institution;
- a share of, or similar interest in, a credit union;
- a share of, or deposit with, a SODEQ in Quebec;
- mortgages for Canadian real estate, including your own mortgage, if certain restrictions are observed, and shares in most mortgage investment corporations;
- debt securities of widely held cooperatives;
- shares and other investments in certain Canadian private small businesses.

Severe penalties apply if non-qualified investments are held in an RRSP.

Although these properties are qualified investments, they may also be considered foreign property. An RRSP can hold no more than 12 per cent (in 1990, increasing by two percentage points annually to reach 20 per cent for 1994 and subsequent taxation years) of the cost of all RRSP property in foreign investments. However, for each $1 invested in qualifying small business securities, an additional $3 can be invested in foreign shares, to a maximum of 20 per cent of the total cost of all RRSP property. Thus, a maximum of 32 per cent of your RRSP could be in foreign investments in 1990.

SPECIAL SITUATIONS

Marriage Breakdown

On the breakdown of a marriage, funds may be transferred from one spouse's RRSP or RRIF to the other spouse's RRSP, RRIF or RPP on a tax-deferred basis. The attribution rules, under which income from property transferred from one spouse to the other is taxed in the hands of the transferor, not the recipient, do not apply to such an RRSP transfer. In addition, the rules discouraging the collapsing of spousal RRSPs do not apply on the breakdown of a marriage.

In order not to be taxed, payments made as a result of marriage breakdown from one person's RRSP to the RRSP of the person's spouse or former spouse must be pursuant to a decree, order or judgment of a competent tribunal or a written separation agreement.

RRSPs and Non-Residents

The tax consequences of becoming a non-resident can be extremely complex. Deciding how to deal with your RRSP should be considered in concert with the many other financial and tax decisions you must make at that time. In very general terms, tax is withheld from many types of payments originating in Canada and made to residents of another country. The other country also may tax the "payment", but most give credit for any Canadian taxes already paid (i.e., withheld at source). The Canadian tax treatment of RRSP amounts generally depends on whether the RRSP has matured, and also on your new country of residence.

If your RRSP has matured, the annuity or RRIF income may qualify as pension income under the tax treaty, if any, Canada has with your new country of residence. For example, under the Canada-United States tax treaty, the annuity payments could qualify as periodic pension payments that are subject to a 15 per cent rate of withholding tax. Under certain other treaties, periodic pension income is exempt from withholding tax. Tax may also be levied in the new country, with credit given for the Canadian withholding tax paid.

If Canada does not have a tax treaty with the foreign country, the withholding rate is 25 per cent. This is also the rate that would normally apply to payments that do not qualify as periodic pension payments, for example, a lump sum withdrawal from an RRSP.

Some countries may tax only the income element in an RRSP annuity or RRIF and ignore the capital element, i.e., the amount in the RRSP used to buy the annuity or RRIF.

If your RRSP has not matured and it is collapsed while you are a non-resident, Canadian withholding tax at the rate of 25 per cent is levied against the entire amount. You may also be subject to tax on the amount in your new country of residence. Many countries do not recognize tax deferral vehicles such as RRSPs and will tax the accumulated income in the RRSP on a current basis, treating it like an ordinary investment account or a trust.

In some situations, you might consider transferring your RRSP to a new plan before leaving Canada, which in effect may step up the cost base of the RRSP, and then collapsing it on taking up residence in the new country, in which case only the 25 per cent withholding tax is paid on the entire amount.

As an alternative to a lump-sum withdrawal, it is possible to withdraw the funds over a period of years. Non-residents have the option of filing an ordinary Canadian tax return and reporting certain types of income, including RRSP amounts, in the normal way. You will be entitled to full personal tax credits. By withdrawing an amount each year from the RRSP on which tax approximately equal to your personal tax credits would be levied, Canadian tax may be avoided provided the ordinary Canadian tax return is filed. (Under a pending technical amendment to be effective for the 1991 taxation year, you will not be able to claim personal tax credits if less than 50 per cent of your income is taxable in Canada.)

If you maintain the RRSP, your new country of residence may ignore it as a tax shelter vehicle and tax you on income earned each year, even though no income is actually received. If you eventually return to Canada and begin receiving an RRSP retirement income here, you will be taxed by Canada and no credit will be given for any foreign tax previously paid.

Creditor Access to Your RRSP

The courts have decided that creditors are able to gain access to a bankrupt's RRSP to settle debts. Only some insurance-type RRSPs offer any creditor protection. However, creditors cannot gain access to life annuity payments, and they may have trouble seizing term certain annuity payments or the funds in an RRIF. Switching your RRSP to an insurance company shortly before you declare bankruptcy probably will not offer any protection, since the bankruptcy laws see through these types of transactions.

RRSPs on Death

The tax treatment of RRSP amounts on the death of the annuitant depends on whether the RRSP had matured and on who is the beneficiary. A spouse receives the most generous treatment. To ensure that RRSP amounts go to the intended beneficiaries with as little trouble as possible, you should name specific RRSP beneficiaries in the RRSP contract or in your will.

If the RRSP has not matured, generally the fair market value of all RRSP property is included in the income of the deceased in the year of death and taxed accordingly in the final income tax return before it is distributed to beneficiaries of the deceased.

However, there are two exceptions. First, if a spouse (which for these purposes includes a common-law spouse who lived with the deceased for at least one year) is named as beneficiary, the plan is essentially transferred to the spouse on a tax-deferred basis.

Second, a "refund of premiums" is not included in the deceased's income. A refund of premiums, which includes all accumulated income, is defined as either:

- any amount so elected and paid to the deceased annuitant's spouse from the RRSP because the spouse was not specifically named as a beneficiary; or
- if the annuitant had no spouse at the time of death, amounts paid to dependent children or grandchildren named as beneficiaries, who were financially dependent on the annuitant.

A spouse, or physically or mentally infirm child, may transfer a refund of premiums to his or her own RRSP or RRIF on a tax-deferred basis in the year of the annuitant's death or within 60 days of the end of that year. In addition, a spouse or a mentally or physically infirm child may purchase a life annuity or term certain annuity to age 90 with the refund of premiums. Other children in receipt of a refund of premiums have no method of deferring tax on the refund of premiums. However, the rate of tax paid by a child on the refund of premiums probably will be lower than the rate paid on the amount by the deceased in the final income tax return; thus, more RRSP funds will be made available to the child.

The legal representative of the deceased's estate may elect for either the spouse or, if there is no spouse, qualifying dependants to receive a refund of premiums.

Somewhat similar rules apply to RRIFs. If the deceased's spouse is the beneficiary, the plan is essentially transferred to the spouse on a tax-deferred basis, and the spouse receives all future payments.

MATURING YOUR RRSP

The decisions to be made before your RRSP matures are not automatic. Careful consideration must be given to your retirement goals, the amount of money that will be required to achieve those goals, and the time at which the money will be required. The tax impact of arranging for your retirement income should also be examined. It is necessary to weigh the RRSP retirement income options carefully. Good RRSP retirement income planning does not just happen. It is the product of careful analysis and forward thinking directed to producing the retirement income you need when you need it. Competent professional advice is recommended when planning for your retirement income.

Maturity Options

RRSPs must be matured before December 31 of the year the annuitant turns 71. Before 1986, RRSPs could not be matured until the annuitant turned age 60. You should ensure that the terms of RRSPs in existence before 1986 are changed to allow for early maturity.

"Maturing" an RRSP simply means arranging to begin receiving a retirement income from accumulated RRSP funds. In the case of some insurance RRSPs, it is simply the date you begin receiving the stipulated RRSP income, assuming you have not notified the issuer otherwise.

With non-insurance RRSPs, there are essentially three maturity options. First, you can arrange to receive an annuity, of which there are several types. Second, you can transfer the accumulated RRSP funds into a registered retirement income fund (RRIF) from which a periodic retirement income is received. Third, you can collapse the RRSP and receive a lump sum after paying the relevant tax.

You can choose any or all of the options and have as many different types of annuities and RRIFs as you want. This flexibility allows you to arrange the type of retirement income you need to suit your expected income requirements. For example, you might consider collapsing a portion of your accumulated RRSPs to finance spending in the early years of your retirement, perhaps for extended travel, although this can also be accomplished with an RRIF. You also probably want to build in a certain amount of inflation protection by transferring some of your RRSP funds to an RRIF and/or indexed annuity.

Even after choosing your retirement income options, RRSPs remain particularly flexible, as you can switch from option to option with relative freedom. For example, you can switch an RRIF to another issuer to earn a better return. As well, you can have as many RRIFs as you like. You can also withdraw any amount from any RRIF at any time, although a minimum amount must be withdrawn from each RRIF each year. You also may be able to commute RRSP annuities, depending on the terms of the contract, in which case the commuted amount becomes taxable. However, amounts withdrawn from an RRIF in excess of the required minimum amount and commuted annuity amounts may be directly transferred on a tax-deferred basis to other annuities or an RRIF, or even to an RRSP if you are under 72. You also may be able to buy an impaired health life annuity from some life insurance companies, which provides for larger payments if you can establish that your life expectancy is considerably shorter than normal, although the same result can be accomplished with an RRIF.

You do not have to acquire an annuity or RRIF from the issuer of your RRSP. Shop around for the best rates on the options you want, and consider using an annuities broker or other professional advisor to search for the best rates and make arrangements for you. Don't forget to assess the role you want to play in managing your retirement income. Setting up a self-directed RRIF may sound like a good idea, but consider whether you will still want to make, or indeed be able to make, investment decisions 15 or 20 years into your retirement.

It is extremely important that you do not wait until the last minute to arrange maturity of your RRSP, i.e., December 31 of the year you turn 71. If you miss the deadline, all accumulated funds in your RRSP are included in income in the year following the year you turn 71, with no recourse for correcting your oversight. Some RRSP issuers, or perhaps your RRSP contract, may provide for automatic maturity, perhaps in the form of a life annuity with a ten-year guarantee, if you do not notify the issuer before the deadline. This at least prevents the RRSP funds from being included in your income, but the life annuity may not suit your retirement needs.

After 1989, you cannot transfer periodic payments from an

annuity purchased with RRSP funds to another RRSP. Many taxpayers under 72 have used this technique to acquire an annuity before the funds are required in order to lock in high interest rate annuities in anticipation that annuity rates will be much lower when they retire. The periodic annuity payments are transferred to another RRSP to offset their inclusion in income for tax purposes. If rates do indeed decline, they have locked in the higher rate on a portion of their RRSP retirement income. If rates stay the same, they are no better or worse off. If rates are higher, they lose out to some extent. However, a similar amount of flexibility should continue to be available under the new rules. If interest rates are low, RRSP funds can be transferred to a RRIF rather than to an annuity. When rates rise, the RRIF amounts can then be transferred to annuities. If you have an RRSP annuity and you expect interest rates to rise substantially, you could commute the annuity, if the contract so allows, and transfer the amount to a RRIF. When rates have peaked, you would then use the RRIF amounts to purchase a more attractive annuity. It is likely that you will be penalized to some extent by the issuer when you commute an annuity. Note that most life annuities cannot be commuted, except on the death of the annuitant.

Early Maturity

Maturing your RRSPs early can be expensive in terms of reduced income. Try to delay maturing your RRSPs until you absolutely must, or mature only a portion of your accumulated RRSP funds at any one time.

If you are 65 or older, RRSP retirement income qualifies for the federal pension income tax credit of 17 per cent of eligible pension income, up to a maximum credit of $170. If one spouse is unable to use all or part of the credit, the unused portion may be transferred to the other spouse.

RRSP Annuities

There are essentially two types of annuities - life and term certain. Under a life annuity, the periodic payments, which you must receive at least once a year, continue until you die. The amount payable is based on the average life expectancy for someone your age and on current interest rates, among other factors. Term certain RRSP annuities are payable to age 90, or to the year your spouse turns 90. Payments cease after your ninetieth year and are based primarily on current interest rates.

Life annuities may have a guaranteed term, usually 10 or 15 years, but not beyond age 90. For such annuities, payments continue to your beneficiaries in the event of your death prior to the end of the guarantee period. In addition, last surviving spouse life annuities may be acquired, which guarantee payments to continue to be made to the surviving spouse.

Both life and term certain annuities may be indexed according to increases in whole or in part in the Consumer Price Index. In practice, these types of annuities are rare, and, if available, they are expensive. More common are annuities that are indexed by a specific factor each year. The maximum increase currently allowed is 4 per cent. You also may opt for an annuity under which the payments change each year, based on the change in value of a specific group of assets maintained by the issuer, or based on changes in generally quoted Canadian market interest rates.

Term annuities can be purchased from either trust companies or insurance companies, while life annuities can be purchased only from insurance companies. RRSP annuity income is taxable in the year it is received.

The table below illustrates the monthly income that a $50,000 investment will produce when invested in various ways at particular ages. The figures were supplied by Polson MacStephen, Retirement Income Specialists, a Toronto-based RRIF/annuity broker.

Monthly incomes shown commence one month after purchase date. The listed incomes are subject to change as interest rates fluctuate, and represent an average of the highest yielding plans at October 1, 1990.

When considering retirement income options, remember that payments in the early years for indexed an-

Age at Purchase	Single Life Annuity (10-Year Guarantee)		Joint Life Annuity (10-Year Guarantee)	Term Certain To Age 90	RRIF to Age 90 (First Year's Income Only)
	Male	Female	Male & Female	Male & Female	Minimum Formula
60	524	502	483	480	140
61	529	505	485	482	145
62	534	509	488	485	150
63	539	512	492	489	156
64	544	517	495	492	162
65	550	521	499	496	168
66	555	526	503	500	175
67	561	532	507	505	183
68	567	538	512	510	191
69	574	544	517	516	200
70	580	551	523	523	210
71	586	558	529	530	221

nuities are considerably lower than those for level payment annuities, but are much higher in later years. It is extremely important that you very carefully assess your income requirements over the long term before committing yourself to any of the options. Unfortunately, many individuals have to choose between providing sufficient income in the years immediately after retiring when they are physically able to enjoy the income the most, and ensuring sufficient income in later years to protect themselves against inflation.

Registered Retirement Income Funds (RRIFs)

RRIFs have a number of advantages over annuities:

- The inflation protection factor can be better controlled than indexed annuities since the size of annual payments is extremely flexible.
- Unusual income requirements in any year can be taken care of since you can withdraw any amount from an RRIF at any time.
- You can control the investments made in the RRIF that generate the retirement income.

- Your estate benefits in that substantial amounts can remain in the RRIF except during the last few years before you reach age 90.
- You can extend RRIF payments past the time you attain age 90 if your spouse is younger and you elect to use your spouse's age in calculating minimum payments out of the RRIF.
- You can convert amounts in an RRIF to a life annuity at any time, giving you protection past age 90, but the conversion cannot be reversed unless the life annuity is purchased through an RRSP and you are under 71.

There are two potential disadvantages to RRIFs. All amounts must be paid out by age 90, at which time the tax shelter aspect disappears. In addition, RRIF funds can be dissipated by bad or risky investing.

An RRIF resembles an RRSP. Funds are invested by the issuer, or the RRIF can be self-directed. Different plans may hold different types of eligible investments, which are broadly similar to those allowed for RRSPs. All amounts in an RRIF remain tax-sheltered until paid out, and investment performance affects the overall value of the plan.

To use an RRIF, funds in your RRSP must be transferred directly to the RRIF before December 31 of the year you turn 71. You may have any number of RRIFs, and funds from any number of RRSPs may be transferred to these RRIFs. An RRIF may be transferred directly from one issuer to another if you are unhappy with the RRIF's performance, and you may acquire annuities with RRIF amounts. You may also have a self-directed RRIF and make your own investment decisions, or use professional money managers by investing RRIF funds in the various types of mutual funds.

A minimum amount must be paid out from the RRIF each year to the annuitant and be included in the annuitant's income for tax purposes. This minimum amount, which normally increases over the years, is a fraction of the total amount in all RRIFs at the beginning of each year, beginning in the first full calendar year you own one or more RRIFs. The fraction is determined as follows:

$$\frac{\text{1 (one)}}{\text{90 minus your age at the beginning of the year or your spouse's age (if elected)}}$$

For example, if you are 65 at the beginning of the first full calendar year you own an RRIF, and the total value of all your RRIFs is $100,000, you must receive a minimum annual payment of $4,000 from the RRIFs, calculated as:

$$\frac{1}{90 - 65} \times \$100{,}000 = \frac{1}{25} \times \$100{,}000 = \$4{,}000$$

If you elect to use your spouse's age in the fraction determining the minimum annual RRIF payment, the election must be made before the first payment is received out of the RRIF, and it cannot later be revoked.

Any number or amount of payments can be received during the year, as long as at least $4,000 in total is received. Payments will continue until the year you turn 90 (89 at beginning of that year), unless you exhaust the funds in the RRIF before that year.

At any point, you may withdraw any amount from any or all of your RRIFs. However, by withdrawing large amounts, you will be reducing the size of payments in future years. Withholding tax is payable on any excess withdrawn over the minimum amount that must be withdrawn in the year. The tax withheld becomes a credit against your tax payable for the year.

The graph on page 114 assumes that an RRIF is purchased for $100,000 on December 31, the first annual payment is received at the end of the next year, and the annuitant is 65 years old at the beginning of that year. The RRIF earns 10 per cent annually. Three situations are compared:

- Minimum required payments are made over the life of the RRIF (A).
- Payments are made to provide a minimum amount of inflation protection by escalating at about 3 per cent to 4 per cent a year (B).

• Payments of $15,000 a year are made for the first seven years and minimum payments are made thereafter (C).

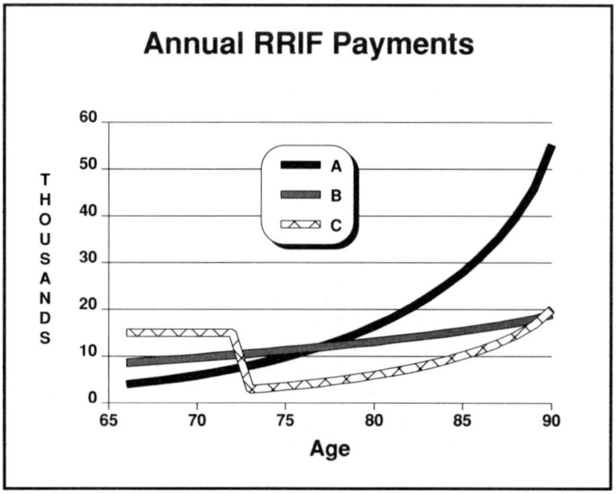

The minimum payment option offers the best inflation protection and tax deferral, but the payments are very small in the early years. The second option offers much larger payments in the early years, but the inflation protection may be inadequate in later years. The third option offers the most income in the early years, but very little income thereafter until the annuitant reaches his or her mid-eighties.

The figures on the graph underscore the importance of choosing the right amount to be paid from your RRIF each year and planning ahead for the next 10, 20, or even 30 years. Opting for large payments in the early years could seriously jeopardize your ability to live comfortably in later years. However, the minimum payment option probably offers more inflation protection than you are ever likely to need.

Virtually everyone should consider putting at least a portion of their RRSP in an RRIF on retirement because of the flexibility of the plans. There is an extremely important election that can be made to designate a spouse to become the "annuitant" on the death of the RRIF owner. Payments will then continue to the spouse and be taxable in the spouse's hands only as each payment is received. If the election is not made, a lump sum is paid to the estate and is taxable on the deceased's final tax return, even if it is the spouse who ultimately receives the lump sum from the estate.

Collapsing Your RRSP

The third RRSP retirement option is distasteful to many because of the tax consequences. If you collapse an RRSP, the entire amount in the particular plan must be brought into income and taxed in that year, often at the highest personal tax rate. Tax must be withheld by the issuer when you collapse an RRSP. The withholding rates are shown in the table in "Withdrawals from an RRSP" earlier in the Chapter. The tax withheld does not represent your actual tax liability; it is simply a payment on account of taxes eventually owing.

If your retirement plans include moving to a foreign country and thus becoming a non-resident of Canada, you may be able to save on Canadian taxes by first establishing your non-resident status and then collapsing your RRSP. Non-resident withholding tax will apply to the funds withdrawn from your RRSP, but this will likely be at a lower rate than the rates outlined above for residents of Canada, particularly if you become a resident of a country with which Canada has a tax treaty providing for a specially reduced rate of withholding.

If you remain resident in Canada, need to use RRSP funds, and want to save tax, average your income by collapsing RRSPs over several years. With only three tax brackets, however, the maximum tax rate is difficult to avoid. Not everyone will save tax by collapsing RRSPs over several years.

Besides paying tax at a high marginal rate when you collapse an RRSP, you also lose the tax deferral that is still available in the RRSP, an RRIF, or even in an annuity. This probably is of little concern if the RRSP is collapsed to satisfy immediate cash requirements.

The major advantage of collapsing an RRSP is that funds can be made available in an amount to suit your needs in the early years of retirement. There does not even have to be an excessive tax cost if you are under age 71 and do not mature your other RRSPs until you absolutely must. However, a similar result can be achieved with an RRIF, possibly at less cost, and it can generally be done more easily.

Retirement Income from Your RRSP

If you do not participate in a company sponsored pension plan, it is likely that an RRSP will be the best way you can save for your retirement. The use of tax-sheltered funds to earn income in your RRSP, especially over a long period of time, provides you with a powerful opportunity to build up your assets before you retire. This will be particularly true as increased annual RRSP contribution limits are phased in. Remember too that when the time comes to mature your RRSP, you should investigate all the options carefully, as the level of your retirement income is at stake.

7. Investing for the Future

$100,000 Capital Gains Exemption

The exemption applies generally to gains from dispositions of all capital property of individuals resident in Canada, including foreign property. Starting in 1988, reserves (that portion of a capital gain not due in the year of disposition of an asset) brought into income that relate to dispositions of capital property after 1984 are eligible for the exemption. The exemption is cumulative over an individual's lifetime to a maximum of $100,000 of capital gains.

Briefly, the exemption is available for capital gains realized in the year net of allowable capital losses of the year and allowable capital losses carried over from other years (an allowable capital loss is currently three-fourths of a capital loss). You can no longer deduct up to $2,000 ($1,000 in Quebec) of allowable capital losses from other income, except that the $2,000 ($1,000 in Quebec) deduction remains for capital losses realized before May 23, 1985, and carried forward. However, the amount of capital gains eligible for the exemption is reduced by any loss so claimed. The amount eligible for exemption is also reduced by the amount of any allowable business investment losses claimed after 1984. You do not have to claim the maximum eligible exemption in any particular year. Any gain must be reported in your tax return for the year in which it is realized; otherwise, the exemption is not available in respect of the gain. The exemption is claimed on FormT657 (Form TP235 in Quebec).

Regarding the lifetime exemption, note that:

- Any gain on disposition of your principal residence is tax-exempt and is not included in your $100,000 capital gains exemption. (See Chapter 2.)
- An additional $400,000 (total $500,000) lifetime exemption is available under special rules for qualified farm property and shares of qualified small business corporations.
- The taxable portion of cash bonuses received on Canada Savings Bonds is treated as interest, rather than as a taxable capital gain (beginning in 1985).
- A portion of the gain on stock options for shares in Canadian- controlled private corporations may not be eligible for the exemption. (See Chapter 2.)

Planning with the $100,000 Capital Gains Exemption

Changing Rules. There have been two fundamental changes to the taxation of capital gains. First, the lifetime exemption was capped at its 1987 level of $100,000 of net capital gains, instead of rising to the $500,000 level originally planned (except for qualified farming property and qualified small business corporation shares).

Second, the inclusion rate for capital gains increased starting in 1988. For 1988 and 1989, the inclusion rate was two-thirds of the net capital gain (up from one-half in 1987). For 1990 and following years, the inclusion rate is three-fourths. As a result, for every $100 of net capital gain, $75 is included in income in 1990 and thereafter. You then may use your capital gains exemption to offset the inclusion. The effect of the inclusion rate and the exemption is that $75,000 of taxable capital gains for 1990 and thereafter can be covered by the exemption (less previously used exemption amounts).

Before realizing capital gains, try to determine whether you are subject to the alternative minimum tax (AMT). Essentially, the non-taxable part of the capital gain (one-fourth after 1989) is added to the regular income base for determining the AMT. Consequently, tax may be payable even if you claim the capital gains exemption in respect of the gain. AMT paid in a particular year may, however, be carried forward seven years and deducted from your ordinary tax liability in excess of any AMT liability for the subsequent year.

Crystallizing the Exemption. You may want to realize capital gains now if you believe that the government may repeal or roll back the capital gains exemption. The result could be a reduction of tax on a future sale. You may be able to crystallize the exemption without actually disposing of the particular asset to an arm's length third party (for example, a properly structured sale to a family member or a holding company).

Doubling Up on the Exemption. Many Canadian families realize more than $100,000 of capital gains in their lifetime, but often the gains are realized almost entirely in the hands of one spouse. Try to have each spouse invest enough personal income to realize sufficient capital gains to use fully the $100,000 exemption. One method might be to have the lower-income spouse invest his or her income while the higher-income spouse pays all household expenses. Remember, tighter income attribution rules (see Chapter 4) have made it extremely difficult to have capital gains realized in your spouse's hands instead of by you.

Capital gains realized by your children on capital assets transferred to them by you are not attributed back to you. Any such transfer is deemed to take place at fair market value, except for certain farm property, which means you must recognize any gain or loss at the time of the transfer. However, any future gain will accrue in the hands of the child.

Capital Gains in Investment Holding Corporations. If you have incorporated your investments in a holding company, you will not benefit when the corporation disposes of securities and capital gains are realized since the capital gains exemption is available only to individuals. You will, of course, benefit when you sell your shares of the investment holding company and realize a gain. In many cases, you will be better off owning securities personally rather than through a holding company. If the accrued gains in the company are small, consider winding up the company to ensure that future gains accumulate directly in your hands. If the accrued gains in the company are large, there may be techniques available for taking advantage of the $100,000 capital gains exemption.

Farm Property. The capital gain deferral on a transfer of farm property to your children is not affected by the capital gains exemption. However, there is no point having your exemption go unused, so it may be more beneficial to sell the property to your children and use the $500,000 exemption. Alternatively, consider structuring a sale to use only $400,000 of the exemption for farms, retaining the other $100,000 exemption for other asset dispositions. A disposition of farm property to your children now requires careful planning to ensure the most beneficial tax treatment.

Capital Gains Election. Because of the $100,000 capital gains exemption, you may want to ensure that all gains are treated as capital gains, not income gains. You may make a once-in-a-lifetime election to have all gains and losses from the disposition of Canadian securities, with certain exceptions, treated as capital gains and losses. Security traders and non-residents, among others, cannot make this election. The election is made on a prescribed form and automatically applies to all future transactions in qualifying Canadian securities.

Think carefully before making this election, however. If you elect to treat all such assets as capital, you may be unable to claim certain expenses related to holding the assets, such as interest on borrowings to purchase them. Also, the election automatically means that losses on the disposition of such assets are capital. This restricts the deductibility of any losses because they can be used only to offset capital gains.

For capital gains not sheltered by the lifetime exemption, the tax advantage versus ordinary income has diminished because the inclusion rate for capital gains has now increased to 75 per cent. Accordingly, it is important to review your long-range expectations before making such an election.

Large Capital Gains Before 1987. Some taxpayers had a problem realizing capital gains in excess of the limits in 1985 and 1986. For example, if you realized an $80,000 capital gain ($40,000 taxable capital gain) in 1986, you were able to claim only $25,000 of the taxable portion under your capital gains exemption assuming no exemption was claimed in 1985. No carry forward of the gain was permitted so the remaining $15,000 was subject to tax in 1986. If, however, you happened to be able to claim a reserve on proceeds not due on the sale of the capital asset, any reserve brought into income in 1988 or future years is eligible for the exemption, provided the capital asset was disposed of after 1984. The reserve is, however, brought into income in 1988 or future years is eligible for the exemption, provided the capital asset was disposed of after 1984. The rcscrvc is, however, brought into income at the inclusion rate for that year (three-fourths after 1989).

United States Real Estate. Gains from the sale of U.S. vacation property are eligible for the $100,000 capital gains exemption, and the property may also qualify as a principal residence. However, even though most capital gains realized by a Canadian resident are exempt from U.S. tax under the Canada-U.S. tax treaty, dispositions of U.S. real property after 1985 are not exempt and can be taxed in the U.S. under the Foreign Investment in Real Property Tax Act (FIRPTA).

If the gain from the disposition of U.S. property is taxed in the U.S., you are entitled to a foreign tax credit in Canada, up to the amount of Canadian tax otherwise due. Essentially, this foreign tax credit should eliminate any Canadian tax liability on the gain. Consequently, it generally will not be beneficial to offset capital gains on U.S. real estate with your lifetime exemption, since the gains are not likely to be subject to significant Canadian tax in any case.

Capital Gains and Losses

The following discussion applies to all taxpayers, but particularly those who will be taxable on their capital gains or who have incurred capital losses.

Allowable capital losses, other than "business investment losses" (see below), offset taxable capital gains in the year. Any unused allowable capital losses can be carried back to the three preceding years, or be carried forward indefinitely to offset taxable capital gains in future years. You may now choose the amount of loss carryovers to use and the year in which you use them. Do not apply losses so that you end up with unused dividend tax credits or other deductions or tax credits.

A loss on transfer of property to a corporation controlled by you or your spouse is deferred until your shares in the corporation are sold. A loss on transfer of property to your RRSP, your RRIF, or your spouse's RRSP is denied completely. Therefore, consider selling the property to realize the loss and then transferring or reinvesting the proceeds, taking care to avoid the superficial loss rules (see below).

Settlement Date. Remember that a disposition of shares through a stock exchange is deemed to take place at "settlement date". For Canadian exchanges, settlement date is five business days after the trading date. This means the last trading date in 1990 could possibly be as early as December 20. However, if the transaction is a cash sale (payment made and share certificates delivered on the trade date), you have until December 31, 1990, to make the trade.

Superficial Loss. You cannot claim a capital loss on an asset you really intend to continue to hold. This rule also applies if the assets are acquired by your spouse or a corporation controlled by you. Thus, where property is sold at a loss and the same asset or "identical" assets are purchased within 30 days before or after the disposition, and the repurchased asset is still held 30 days after the original disposition, a "superficial loss" results. The person acquiring the replacement asset adds the loss to his or her cost base and the seller of the asset is denied the loss. The rule does not apply if the assets are acquired by your children or parents.

For example, assume you had an asset that cost $3,000 and sold it for $1,000, and then repurchased an identical asset for $1,100 within 30 days either before or after the sale. Instead of having a capital loss of $2,000, the capital loss would be added to the cost of the asset repurchased, so that the new asset would have a cost base of $3,100, assuming you still owned the asset 31 days after the disposition.

If the asset is repurchased more than 30 days before or after the disposition, the rule will not apply. Thus, in our example there would be a capital loss of $2,000, and the new asset would have a cost base of only $1,100.

Identical Properties. Capital properties of a similar kind are subject to special rules covering "identical properties". Stocks of the same class, or bonds of substantially identical characteristics of the same corporation, are "identical properties". These assets are "pooled" and lose their specific identities.

In 1990, if 200 shares of a stock are purchased for $8 per share and, subsequently, 100 shares are purchased for $11 per share, the tax cost of the shares is considered to be $9 per share ($2,700/300). If the 100 shares purchased for $11 are sold the next day at the same price, you will have a capital gain of $2 per share, which will result in $150 (three-fourths of $200) being included in income in 1990.

Where identical properties are owned at the end of 1971 and additional purchases are made thereafter (a common situation with dividend reinvestment plans or where stock options are regularly exercised), complications arise. Properties owned at the end of 1971 are pooled separately from those acquired later, and the formula for determining their cost bases differs. Generally, pre-1972 properties are considered to be sold before post-1971 properties.

Cumulative Net Investment Losses

Starting in 1988, net capital gains eligible for the capital gains exemption are reduced by all cumulative net investment losses (CNILs) deducted in computing income for taxation years after 1987. Your CNIL at the end of a year is the amount by which your accumulated investment expenses essentially exceed your accumulated investment income. Your investment expenses essentially consist of the following items that have been deducted in computing your income for the 1988 and subsequent taxation years:

- Deductions claimed with respect to property that will yield interest, dividends, rent or other income from property. Such deductions include interest, safe deposit box rental, other carrying charges, capital cost allowance (CCA), and so forth.
- Carrying charges, including interest, with respect to an interest in, or a contribution to, a limited partnership (unless you

are the general partner) or any other partnership where you are not actively engaged in the business of the partnership (unless you carry on a similar business).
- Your share of a loss (except allowable capital losses) of any partnership described above.
- Fifty per cent of your share of deductions attributed to a resource flow-through share or relating to Canadian exploration and other resource expenses of a partnership where you are not actively engaged in the business.
- Any loss for the year from property or from the renting or leasing of real property (including a MURB) owned by you or a partnership, not otherwise included in investment expenses. (However, CCA claims before 1989 for certified film production are not included in investment expenses.)

Your investment income for a year essentially consists of the following items that are included in computing income for the year:

- Interest, taxable dividends, rent and other income from property (including recaptured depreciation in respect of items generating income from property).
- Your share of the income (including recaptured depreciation but not including taxable capital gains) from most limited partnerships or other partnerships where you are not actively engaged in the business of the partnership (unless you carry on a similar business).
- Income (including recaptured depreciation) for the year from property or from the renting or leasing of real property owned by you or a partnership not otherwise included.
- Fifty per cent of recovered exploration and development expenses included in income.

Whether or not your capital gains qualify for the capital gains exemption, you are still able to deduct the interest paid on funds you borrow for investment purposes. The CNIL rules are concerned only with the calculation of your capital gains exemption. You need not be concerned with them if you have exhausted your capital gains exemption.

Application of the Rules. Assume that you borrow $20,000 in December 1990 at an annual interest cost of $2,000. You use the funds to buy shares of a public corporation that pays no dividends. Exactly two years later, you sell the shares for $30,000 and pay off the loan. You have a taxable capital gain of $7,500 (three-quarters of the $10,000 gain), which must be included in income. Unfortunately, the maximum capital gains exemption you can claim is only $3,500 ($7,500 less your $4,000 CNIL). The $4,000 difference remains in your income and is subject to tax at your marginal tax rate.

Your net investment loss is not calculated on an investment-by-investment basis, nor on an annual basis, but rather on a cumulative and pooled basis after 1987 for all of your investment assets. Carrying charges associated with one security may therefore reduce your capital gains exemption available to offset a taxable capital gain realized on the sale of another security. The CNIL rules do not erode your lifetime capital gains exemption, but they can delay your use of all or part of it to future years in which your cumulative investment income exceeds your cumulative investment expenses.

Planning Strategies. Obviously, you want to avoid having the CNIL rules delay your use of the lifetime capital gains exemption after 1987. If you incur interest expense after 1987 on money borrowed for investment purposes, and your investments yield only capital gains, the rules limit access to your capital gains exemption in respect of those investments, and accordingly, part of the capital gains becomes taxable. You may still want to borrow in this situation if the investment looks as if it will produce large capital gains, but you should keep the CNIL rules in mind. If you do borrow, consider borrowing first for business, and then, only if necessary, for investment. The interest expense on funds you use to carry on an unincorporated business or profession does not enter into the CNIL calculation.

If you own a company, consider receiving dividends or interest from the company in order to reduce or eliminate the CNIL balance. Also, if you invest in tax shelters, consider whether it may be advantageous to hold these investments in your company. The CNIL rules do not apply to the company.

Since there are a number of factors to consider before applying these planning strategies, you should consult your professional tax advisor.

Business Investment Losses

A business investment loss is the loss incurred on the disposition of shares in a small business corporation (a defined term) or on the disposition of most forms of debt owed to you by a small business corporation. A business investment loss may be used to reduce income from other sources.

Shares or debt must be disposed of to a person with whom you deal at arm's length. Shares also will be considered disposed of if the corporation is bankrupt (or in some circumstances if it has ceased to carry on business), and debt will be considered disposed of if the debt is established to be uncollectible. If the shares disposed of were issued prior to 1972 (or were substituted for such shares), the business investment loss must be reduced by the amount of any taxable dividends received on the shares (or substituted shares) by the taxpayer, the taxpayer's spouse, or a trust of which either was a beneficiary. The amount subtracted is eligible for regular capital loss treatment. This dividend rule does not apply if you have acquired such pre-1972 shares at arm's length after 1971.

Three-fourths of the business investment loss, the "allowable business investment loss" (ABIL), is treated in the same manner as a non-capital loss, such as a business loss. This means that you must deduct the allowable portion from all sources of income in the current taxation year. Unused losses may be carried back three years and forward for seven years. Income in the loss year must be reduced to zero before these losses can be carried backward or forward, with the result that personal tax credits are lost. However, you now have a choice as to how much of a loss carryover you want to claim in a carryover year. After the seven-year carryforward period, unused allowable business investment losses become ordinary capital losses and may be carried forward indefinitely.

A taxpayer's business investment loss for a taxation year after 1985 is treated as an ordinary capital loss to the extent of any claims made under the lifetime capital gains exemption in previous years. In addition, any capital gain realized is not eligible for the capital gains exemption to the extent of any business investment losses realized by the taxpayer in prior years after 1984.

Reserves for Proceeds Not Yet Due

With the capital gains exemption, taxpayers will be using the reserve mechanism relatively seldom, at least until they use up their limit on the exemption. Originally, reserves claimed in a previous year and later brought into income were not eligible for the exemption except in the case of post-1984 dispositions of farm property. A reserve brought into income after 1987 (that relates to a disposition after 1984) is, however, eligible for the lifetime capital gains exemption.

If a capital asset is sold, giving rise to a capital gain, and the full amount of the proceeds is not due by the end of the year, a part of the capital gain may be deferred by claiming a reserve for the proceeds not yet due. The amounts brought into income each year are treated as ordinary capital gains. The includible amounts will be based on the inclusion rate in the year the reserve is brought into income (not the inclusion rate in the year the asset was sold).

The capital gains reserve provisions are restricted. The old reserve provisions affect all dispositions made on or before November 12, 1981, and also dispositions of capital property after that date if the sale was pursuant to a written agreement entered into on or before November 12, 1981. The current rules apply to dispositions after November 12, 1981, if not evidenced in writing as being underway on or before that date. Note that you may claim less than the maximum available reserve in any year.

Current Rules. You may claim a reserve over a five-year period, based on the lesser of two amounts. The first is an amount equal to the portion of the gain reasonably attributable to the proceeds not yet due. The second amount is determined according to the one-fifth rule, under which at least one-fifth of the gain on a cumulative basis must be brought into income in the year of sale and each of the immediately succeeding four years.

A ten-year reserve, instead of a five-year reserve, is allowed on the transfer of farm property, shares in a family farm corporation, or shares in a small business corporation to your child, grandchild, or great-grandchild (resident in Canada).

Old Reserves. For dispositions of capital property on or before November 12, 1981, the old reserve rules apply, which allow you to claim a reserve based on the proceeds method only over the number of years the proceeds remain outstanding.

If you claim a smaller reserve than the maximum allowed under either the old or new rules in any particular year, you cannot claim a larger reserve in the next year.

Special Bonuses on Canada Savings Bonds

You may be holding CSBs on which the federal government pays a special cash bonus. Such bonuses are treated as interest, not as capital gains, but only one-half of the bonus is included in income. If you are still holding such bonds, you should cash them as soon as possible. The last series matured on November 1, 1987, and no longer pays interest.

CSBs issued before 1981 pay interest above the rate stated on the bond. This excess interest is considered to be a cash bonus, half of which is treated as taxable interest. Details are available where you bank.

CSBs issued after 1980 (Series 36 and subsequent) do not carry a bonus. Instead, the interest rate is adjusted annually.

Dividends

Dividends are grossed up by 25 per cent, and the dividend tax credit is 16.67 per cent of the cash amount of dividends received. The following example shows how a top bracket taxpayer with federal tax payable in excess of $15,000 is taxed on a $1,000 dividend received in 1990 and 1991.

	1990	**1991**
Cash dividend	$1,000	$1,000
Gross-up	250	250
	1,250	1,250
Federal tax (29%)	363	363
Dividend tax credit	(167)	(167)
	196	196
Surtaxes	16	20

Provincial tax (assumed @ 55%)	108	108
Total tax	$ 320	$ 324
Amount retained after tax	$ 680	$ 676

An individual with no dependants and with only dividend income could receive approximately $22,700 of dividends in 1990 without paying tax.

Interest

The investment income deduction, under which you could formerly shelter interest and dividend income, ended December 31, 1987. Now, even trifling amounts of interest income earned on your bank savings account are taxable. If you are in the top tax bracket and therefore pay combined federal and provincial tax of about 46 per cent (depending on the province where you reside), you now lose 46 cents of every dollar of interest you earn. That may make it tough to stay ahead of inflation, so shop carefully when you acquire interest-bearing investments.

Although interest income is generally taxable when it is received, there used to be rules that required interest income to be accrued every three years, whether it was received or not. However, for interest-bearing investments acquired after 1989, interest income must be reported annually. If you own pre-1990 investments on which interest accrues but is not payable, you may still report the interest income every three years as opposed to annually.

Investing in Tax Shelters

Many upper income Canadians have discovered the hard way that the "quality of investment" aspect of a shelter is by far the most important element, overshadowing all other considerations, including immediate tax savings. Receiving a deduction for the money you put into a tax shelter is no consolation if you end up losing your money because the investment is a bad one.

Investment opportunities, rather than tax savings, should be the primary, and usually the only, motivation for making a tax shelter investment. If you are considering investing in a tax shelter, you should obtain professional advice before committing your funds and future state of mind to these high risk investments.

Limited Partnerships. The investment tax credits and losses claimed by limited partners are limited to the extent that their investment in the partnership is at risk. The amount at risk for the first purchaser is generally the adjusted cost base of his or her partnership interest at the end of the year plus any partnership income distributed. This amount is reduced by any amount owing to the partnership and any guarantee or indemnity provided to protect the limited partner against the loss of his or her investment. Despite the strict rules, limited partnerships are still used to structure business deals because they frequently offer a good way of arranging financing and limiting risk. A number of transitional rules apply, but generally limited partnerships in existence on February 25, 1986, and those in the course of raising capital on this date, are exempt from the current rules.

Mineral Exploration and Oil and Gas Shelters. With flow-through shares, the various deductions and tax credits associated with oil and gas drilling and mineral exploration flow through directly to shareholders.

Research and Development (R&D) Shelters. Few shelters are available. The most popular form of investing, limited partnerships, has been severely curtailed. The Government has issued a comprehensive definition of scientific research that qualifies for maximum R&D deductions.

Multiple-Unit Residential Buildings (MURBs). The MURB program was cancelled in 1981, and tax reform eliminated the MURB as a tax shelter. Generally, for units acquired from arm's length parties after June 17, 1987, capital cost allowance may not be claimed to create or increase a rental loss. If you acquired your MURB before June 18, 1987 (or after June 17, 1987, pursuant to an agreement in writing entered into before June 18, 1987), you may continue to claim capital cost allowance to increase or create losses only until 1993. Starting in 1994, MURBs will be treated in the same way as other rental properties owned by persons not actively engaged in the real estate business. Thus, capital cost allowance can be used only to reduce rental income to zero, but not to create a loss deductible against other income.

Canadian Films. In 1987, you could claim the total cost of an investment in a certified Canadian film production as capital cost allowance over two years. Tax reform changed this to 30 per cent per year, calculated on a declining balance basis, disregarding the half-year rule. In addition, a further deduction is granted when the yearly income earned from Canadian film productions is sufficient. The change is effective generally for investments acquired after 1987.

Farming as a Tax Shelter. Depending on the crop or product raised, farming may be a viable tax shelter, but the farm industry itself may be subject to low commodity prices. As well, most taxpayers will be subject to the restricted farm loss rules that limit deductible losses in a year to $8,750 ($5,000 for taxation years commencing before 1989). Farming may be attractive because of the $500,000 capital gains exemption available for gains on qualifying farm property.

Provincial Tax Shelters. Many of the provinces provide incentives to encourage investment in certain areas or industries. For example, some provinces have stock savings plans that provide for tax credits, and some also have venture capital plans to encourage investment in small to medium-size companies.

8. Owner-Managed Private Companies

If you own your own business, you may wonder whether to operate in corporate or unincorporated form. Traditionally, the Canadian income tax system has favoured incorporated Canadian small businesses. The basic calculations regarding income and deductions remain essentially the same as for your unincorporated business. (You should refer to the various sections in the book for details regarding income, deductions, autos and so forth.) There are some differences, however, in the structure of corporate taxation and in planning opportunities through corporations.

Corporation Defined

A corporation is an artificial person created by law. A corporation will have the following characteristics:

- it is a separate legal entity that has an ongoing existence and the ability to contract, i.e., buy, sell, employ, borrow, loan, and own property;
- it must act through individuals;
- ownership is represented by shareholders who also may be employees;

- profits are distributed by dividends, which are taxed in the hands of the shareholders;
- it is a separate taxable entity and must file returns and pay taxes.

Corporate Taxation – Basics

If you run your business as a sole proprietorship, you include the income from the business on your personal tax return, as discussed in Chapter 2. A corporation, on the other hand, is a separate taxable entity. The corporation must file its own tax return and make its own tax instalments. You will include income from the corporation on your personal tax return only when you receive distributions from your corporation in the form of salary, dividends, interest, or some other form of payment.

Similar to the individual rate structure, the corporate structure varies based on the province where the corporate income is generated. In addition, however, the tax rate varies based on the type and amount of income.

The basic federal income tax rate for corporations is 38 per cent effective July 1, 1988. This rate is decreased to 28 per cent on income earned in Canada to accommodate provincial and territorial taxation on such income. A further deduction from the basic tax rate is available for income generated from manufacturing and processing activities (M&P) performed in Canada. The M&P deduction is 4 percentage points since July 1, 1990, and reduces the federal corporate rate to 24 per cent. The M&P deduction will be 5 percentage points as of July 1, 1991, at which time the federal rate on manufacturing and processing income will be 23 per cent.

There also is a federal surtax imposed of 3 per cent of the net federal rate, which increases the federal tax rate for income earned in a province from 28 per cent to 28.84 per cent without the M&P deduction and from 24 per cent to 24.84 per cent with the M&P deduction.

Special tax treatment is provided if your company is a Canadian-controlled private corporation (CCPC). Basically, a CCPC is a resident Canadian corporation, controlled by Canadian residents (other than public corporations). Generally, this control will exist if such Canadian residents hold at least 50 per cent of the voting rights in the company.

However, this is not always the case. When a person has any direct or indirect influence that, if exercised, would result in control in fact of the corporation, he or she is considered to have control of the corporation. For example, a person who holds 49 per cent of the votes of a corporation may be considered to control it where the balance of the votes is widely dispersed among employees of the corporation or is held by a person who could reasonably be considered to act in accordance with the wishes of the person holding the 49 per cent voting interest.

A CCPC is eligible for a federal tax rate reduction (the small business deduction - SBD) on up to $200,000 of active business income annually. (If the company's tax year is less than 12 months, this amount must be prorated.)

The annual $200,000 limit must be shared by "associated corporations" in order to prevent taxpayers from abusing this SBD by forming several corporations to multiply the $200,000 eligible for the reduced rate. Generally, associated corporations are corporations controlled by the same person or group of persons. Thus, it is not possible to set up several corporations and obtain the benefits of the SBD on $200,000 of income for each of them. It also is important to note the requirement that the income be "active business income". If you incorporate your investment portfolio, you will not qualify for the small business deduction because the income generated will not be active business income.

The federal small business deduction (SBD) is 16 percentage points. There is no M&P deduction for income eligible for the SBD. Therefore, if your company is a CCPC generating income from an active business in Canada, the federal corporate tax rate will be 12 per cent for the first $200,000 of taxable income. For income in excess of the $200,000, tax rates normally applicable to all corporations apply as noted above. When you include the 3 per cent federal surtax, the federal income tax rate is 12.84 per cent.

In addition to the federal corporate tax, all provinces also impose income taxes. The provincial tax rates vary from nil to

17 per cent depending on the province, whether there is an M&P deduction, whether there is a small business deduction, and whether the province grants a tax holiday (often for new corporations). Combined federal and provincial corporate income tax rates, therefore, vary considerably depending on the circumstances.

The federal government has proposed a "Large Corporations Tax". This new tax, which is effective from July 1, 1989, received Royal Assent just before this book went to press. The tax is imposed at a rate of 0.175 per cent on a corporation's capital employed in Canada in excess of $10 million. When the GST goes into effect, the rate will be 0.2 per cent starting January 1, 1991. With such a large threshold, most small businesses will not be subject to the LCT. Any LCT liability can be used to offset the corporation's 3 per cent surtax and unused amounts can be carried over. Unlike provincial capital taxes, the LCT cannot be deducted in computing income subject to income tax.

Tax Deferral

For small companies, the combined federal-provincial corporate tax rate can be as low as 12.84 per cent. Even in high-tax provinces, the maximum rate for small companies is only 22.84 per cent. In Quebec, the combined rate is 16.29 per cent. If you compare these rates to those reproduced in Chapter 12 for individuals, you see that the small company rates are significantly lower.

If you operate your business in unincorporated form, you will include the income from the business in your personal tax return as it is earned. Thus, you will pay tax on your business income at your personal marginal tax rate. If you incorporate your business, you initially pay only the corporate tax rate. You will not pay individual tax on the corporate earnings unless you receive distributions in the form of salary, interest or dividends. If you are expanding your business, you will want to retain earnings in the company for that growth. By incorporating your operations, you are able to defer the personal tax on the portion of earnings retained in the business.

For example, if you earn $1,000 of pre-tax income, you would pay about $505 in individual taxes at the top marginal rates. That would leave $495 for reinvestment in the business. If the $1,000 were generated by a corporation eligible for the SBD, the maximum corporate tax would be about $165, leaving $835 for reinvestment. No individual tax would be due until earnings were distributed to shareholders. Thus, in this example, as much as $340 ($505 - $165) of tax might be deferred.

Setting Up the Corporation

Generally, you can transfer your business assets to a corporation without any tax consequences, subject to certain restrictions. In return, the corporation must issue shares to you. You may choose to have part of your investment in the corporation in the form of debt rather than shares. By holding some debt, you have the opportunity to draw earnings out of the corporation as interest, which is tax deductible to the company, as well as drawing earnings out as dividends.

Taxation of Distributions from the Corporation

When you receive payments from the corporation, the tax treatment depends on the nature of the payment. Salary you receive as an employee of your corporation is fully includible in your income in the year of receipt. If you have financed your company partially by loaning the company money, interest payments on such debt also are fully includible in your income. If you have leased assets to the corporation, lease payments paid to you would be included in your income when received, and so forth. All such payments would be deductible in calculating the corporation's income.

It is possible to achieve limited deferral through loans or by leasing assets to your company. If your corporation computes taxable income on the accrual basis (i.e., income is reported as it is earned rather than when it is received, and expenses are reported as incurred rather than as paid), the corporation can record and deduct the interest and rental amounts. These amounts do not have to be included in your taxable income until they actually are paid to you. As a result, you can obtain a tax deduction for the corporation prior to when you have to pay the individual tax on the payments.

There are some restrictions on this deferral ability regarding delays for accrued payables. If they are not paid by the end of the corporation's second taxation year following the accrual, it could result in a double taxation of the amount in question, i.e., a disallowance of the deduction to the corporation while the income to you remains taxable.

It also may be possible to achieve limited deferral through the payment of salaries or bonuses. In such a case, for the corporation to obtain a deduction in the year the salaries or bonuses were accrued, these amounts must be paid within 180 days after the corporation's year-end. When they are paid, you will include them in your taxable income. However, if the corporate year end is after July 5 (i.e., a July 31 year end or later), the amounts can be paid within 180 days, but in the following calendar year. This provides about six months of tax deferral benefit.

Integration

Although you may own most or all of the shares of a corporation, both you and the corporation are separate taxpayers. The corporation pays income tax when profits are earned. When the after-tax profits are distributed from the company as dividends, they are included in your income and the company does not receive a deduction. Consequently, profits generated through a corporation are taxed twice, once when earned by the company and again when distributed as dividends to the shareholders.

To alleviate this double taxation of income earned through a corporation, the corporate and individual tax systems are integrated. This integration is accomplished by grossing up the dividend received by the shareholder to approximate the amount earned before tax at the corporate level. A tax credit is then granted in an amount designed to give the shareholder a credit for the amount of tax already paid by the corporation.

Accordingly, if you receive a dividend distribution from your company, the dividend is included in your income. You also will include an additional 25 per cent of the dividend in your income (to "gross up" the dividend). After you calculate your federal income tax (before calculating the surtax of 8 per cent in 1990 and 10 per cent in 1991), you will take a dividend tax credit equal to two-thirds of the amount by which you grossed up the dividend payment. For Quebec taxes, the dividend tax credit is 44 per cent of the dividend gross-up.

For example:

Dividend received	$100
Dividend gross-up (25% × $100)	25
Taxable income	$125
Federal tax at 29%	$ 36.25
Dividend tax credit (2/3 × $25)	(16.67)
Federal surtax [8% × ($36.25-$16.67)]	1.57
Total federal tax	$ 21.15
Provincial tax [55% assumed rate × ($36.25-$16.67)]	10.77
Total individual tax on dividend	$ 31.92

The integration system is rough justice designed to approximate an individual receiving dividends from a corporation that has enjoyed the small business deduction. To have perfect integration, the federal and provincial combined corporate rate must be 20 per cent, there must be no surtaxes, and the individual must have a provincial tax rate of 50 per cent. Under these conditions, there will be no difference between earning business income through a corporation or directly, as demonstrated in the following example (which assumes a taxpayer in the highest tax bracket).

	Income Earned Directly	Income Earned Through a Corporation
Corporate income		$100
Corporate tax		20
After-tax profits		$ 80
Individual income		
Business profits	$100	

Dividend		$ 80
Dividend gross-up (25% × $80)		20
Taxable income	$100	$100
Federal tax at 29%	$ 29	$ 29
Dividend tax credit (⅔ × $20)	- 0 -	(13.33)
Provincial tax at 50%	14.50	7.83
Total individual tax	43.50	23.50
Corporate tax	- 0 -	20.00
Total tax on $100 income	$ 43.50	$ 43.50

To the extent that the tax rates differ from these hypothetical rates, there will be differences in total taxes paid depending on whether the income is earned directly by an individual or through a corporation. If the corporate tax rate and/or individual tax rates are lower than these hypothetical rates, the total tax paid on income earned through the corporate structure is likely to be less than the total tax that would be paid if the income were earned directly by the individual. To the extent the corporate tax rates are higher than for a small business corporation, there will be a shortfall in relief from double taxation.

Advantages and Disadvantages of Incorporating Your Business

The trade-offs between the corporate and unincorporated structures depend to a great extent on the nature of your activities and the income generated. To determine the tax differential, you must review the differences between the corporate and individual tax rates for the province in which the activities arise. In many cases, however, it will be advantageous to have a corporate structure.

Generally, the tax and non-tax advantages to incorporating your business include:

1. Limited Liability. Because the corporation is a separate legal entity, individual shareholders are not responsible for corporate debts or other liabilities. This may not be an advantage for a small business, because it is common for lending institutions to request personal guarantees on loans to such a corporation. However, your liability remains limited for such things as lawsuits, unless you are personally negligent.

2. Tax Savings or Deferral. As mentioned above, there may be tax savings opportunities and tax deferral opportunities. The savings or deferral opportunities are of particular value to a business that will be investing to expand. The extent of these opportunities depends on the comparative corporate and individual tax rates in the particular circumstances, as well as on the nature of the income earned.

3. Income Splitting and Estate Planning. There are income splitting and estate planning opportunities available through a corporate structure that are not available with an unincorporated business. Some of these are reviewed in Chapters 4 and 10.

4. Levelling of Income. It is possible to achieve a levelling of personal income through control of salary and dividends to avoid high and low income periods, particularly in a business where profits fluctuate from year to year.

5. Pension Plans. A shareholder who is also an employee of the corporation may participate in the company's registered pension plan (RPP). A sole proprietor may not participate in an RPP. Even with increased contribution limits for Registered Retirement Savings Plans (see Chapter 6), the contribution limits for RPPs are potentially higher until the new system of tax assistance for retirement saving is fully implemented. This offers an additional advantage to the corporate structure. There also are other types of fringe benefits such as group term life insurance plans and group sickness or accident insurance plans that may be available to you as an employee of your company, but are not available if your business is unincorporated.

6. Capital Gains Exemption. The corporate structure permits access to an enhanced capital gains exemption on the sale of shares of the corporation running the business. There is an increased capital gains exemption available to holders of shares of a small business corporation (which is not available if the business is unincorporated). This exemption is $500,000. (You should note that it is not in addition to the regular $100,000 capital gains exemption. The total exemption available if you dispose of both small business corporation shares and other capital property is $500,000.)

A "small business corporation" is a CCPC that uses all or substantially all (more than 90 per cent, according to Revenue Canada) of the fair market value of its assets in an active business carried on primarily in Canada. The shares of a Canadian holding company also qualify if substantially all of its assets are shares or debt of other small business corporations. To qualify for the $500,000 exemption, the corporation must be a small business corporation at the time of the sale and the shares must not have been held by anyone other than the seller, or related persons, within the 24 months preceding the sale. In addition, throughout the 24-month period, more than 50 per cent of the fair market value of the assets of the corporation must be used in an active business carried on primarily in Canada in order for the $500,000 exemption to be available. (For a holding company, the qualifying tests for small business status are more stringent.)

Disadvantages of the corporate structure include:

1. **Losses.** A corporation is unable to use losses to offset income generated by the individual. If you generate losses through an unincorporated business, you may use these losses to offset income from other activities. Because the corporation is a separate entity, neither the income nor the losses flow directly to your individual tax return. As a result, you cannot use these losses to offset other types of income. If the corporation generates income in other years, the losses may offset such other income of the corporation (business losses of the corporation may be carried back three years and forward seven years to offset other income of the corporation). Note that if your corporation is generating a loss, the reported loss can be adjusted by reducing your salary payments and substituting dividends.

2. **Costs of Incorporating.** There are additional costs to setting

up and maintaining a corporation that you would not incur with an unincorporated business. Such costs include the initial expenses of preparing the legal documents and taxes such as provincial capital taxes. Ongoing costs include filing forms such as tax returns, holding meetings, maintaining corporate records, and so forth.

3. Capital Taxes. The federal government recently introduced a tax on capital and a number of the provinces have had such a tax for years. The federal capital tax liability is usually eliminated or substantially reduced for small corporations.

Planning with Your Owner-Managed Corporation

There are several aspects of planning that should be reviewed if you have incorporated your business. It is important to keep in mind non-tax factors while developing your plan, however. You need to consider your cash needs and the cash needs of the company. In addition, you must review all your other sources of income, and your position regarding investment income, capital gains, and investment losses. All these factors should be considered when you are reviewing your tax planning for your company.

Payment of Investment Income

One aspect you may want to review is your position under the cumulative net investment loss (CNIL) rules discussed in Chapter 7. If you have cumulative net investment losses, you may want to receive interest or dividend income from your corporation. This income would be netted against any investment losses to reduce the amount of your CNIL. In this manner, the potential restriction of your capital gains exemption can be avoided.

Spousal Salaries

You also may want to consider the payment of a salary to your spouse or other family members. It is necessary that the person actually perform some services for the company, that there be a bona fide employer-employee relationship, and that you be able to support the salary as reasonable. A salary generally will be considered reasonable if a reasonable businessman would have paid the salary under similar circumstances and it is commensurate with the value of the responsibilities assumed and the services performed.

Under these conditions, the corporation will obtain a deduction for the salary payment, and you will have achieved additional income splitting. This salary payment also may open the opportunity for increased contributions to retirement savings plans for that family member.

Salary/Dividend Trade-offs

Probably one of the largest areas of planning for the owner-managed corporation is the determination of the appropriate split between salary payments and dividend payments for the owner-manager.

In theory, it is not supposed to matter whether you draw a salary or a dividend provided the company's taxable income (and that of all associated companies, prorated for any tax years less than 12 months) is not more than $200,000. Salary reduces corporate income tax payable, but the salary then is subject to personal tax. Although a dividend does not reduce corporate tax, the dividend tax credit means less personal tax is paid than on salary income.

Similar to the example presented above regarding integration, this theory is effective only when the combined federal and provincial corporate rate is 20 per cent, there are no surtaxes, and the individual is in a 29 per cent federal tax bracket in a province imposing tax at 50 per cent of the federal rate. In such a case, if 100 per cent of after-tax corporate income is distributed, the total tax would be identical whether it is distributed as salary or dividends. (For every $100 of corporate income the numbers would be identical to the previous example.)

The theory is fine, but the system does not work exactly in the way it was intended. While in many provinces drawing a salary and maximizing RRSP contributions will be preferable to drawing a dividend, this is not true for all provinces nor for all types of business activities. It is generally advisable to withdraw at least as much from the company as possible until the net amount of tax you pay is equal to the tax the company would have paid had you not withdrawn the funds. Depending on your particular circumstances, the best way to do this may be taking all salary, or a combination of salary and dividends. You can loan funds back to the company, and at any time in the future the company can repay the loan to you on a tax-free basis.

The above comments, however, assume that the corporation (and all associated companies, etc.) generates active business income of $200,000 or less. Thus, the full amount of taxable income would be eligible for the small business deduction. If there is taxable income in the corporation in excess of this $200,000, the small business deduction does not apply to this excess, and the corporate tax rate will be considerably higher. Accordingly, it is generally advisable to keep the taxable income of the corporate group at or below $200,000. The most common way of achieving this goal is through salary payments to you as the owner-manager.

This salary will be included in your taxable income in the year of receipt. Recall, however, that in certain cases you may obtain the deduction for the corporation in a year earlier than the year in which you actually receive the payment. There may be a slight deferral advantage to leaving income in the corporation, but the total tax is likely to be higher than if salaries were paid.

Another aspect of the salary payment is that it is important to try to maximize the amounts that you can contribute under the Canada/Quebec Pension Plan and Registered Retirement Savings Plans. These plans have contribution limits based on your earned income for the year. As a result, even though the corporate income may be less than $200,000 without additional salaries or bonuses, you may want to pay enough salary to yourself to maximize your contributions to such plans, providing you have not fully used your pension amount in a companypension plan.

It is important to note that the 1991 contribution limit for RRSPs will be based on 1990 earned income. Consequently, although you can contribute the maximum amount to your

RRSP for 1990 with earned income of $37,500, your 1990 earned income must be at least $63,888.88 in order to contribute the maximum amount ($11,500) to your RRSP for 1991.

It must be noted that for salaries to be deductible by the corporation, they must be "reasonable". What constitutes a reasonable salary is generally a question of fact. However, as a rule the tax authorities do not question the payment of a salary or bonus to a shareholder manager provided payroll tax withholdings are paid.

Selling Your Business

If your business is unincorporated, and you are contemplating a sale of the business, you can in most cases transfer the assets to a corporation and then immediately sell the shares of the corporation to take advantage of the $500,000 capital gains exemption.

If your business is incorporated, but does not qualify as a small business corporation, it may be possible to purify the corporation by removing non-qualified assets from the company. With careful planning, this removal could be effected on a tax-free basis. Generally, however, the purification process should begin long before a sale is being contemplated. There is a provision that could deny the capital gains exemption on a sale of shares of a corporation if appreciated assets have been removed from the corporation on a tax-free basis as part of the sale process.

If you are expecting to sell the shares of your company, you could consider accumulating income in the company to increase the gain. This must be done carefully, however, because to maintain the small business corporation status, substantially all (over 90 per cent, according to Revenue Canada) of the assets, based on fair market values as noted above, must be used in carrying on the corporation's business. As a result, you could not accumulate earnings in the corporation and use those earnings to buy passive investments if such investments will constitute more than 10 per cent of the total fair market value of the corporate assets at the time of sale (or more than 50 per cent for the preceding 24 months, as discussed earlier).

However, you may be able to use the earnings to reduce the corporation's debts and other liabilities.

You may find that when you are negotiating the sale of your business, the buyer may prefer to buy the assets of the company, rather than buying your shares. This provides the buyer with tax write-offs that would be unavailable if the buyer purchased the shares. On your part, the preference will be for a sale of the shares because of the capital gains exemption and the possibilities for spreading exemptions within your family if you previously have organized the share structure to permit ownership by your spouse and children (see the discussion following).

There is room for negotiation. If the disposition qualifies for the $500,000 capital gains exemption, you should be able to negotiate a deal with a purchaser that permits both of you to share the tax benefits from your expanded capital gains exemption. In addition, as a result of recent tax changes, the benefits to the purchaser from acquiring assets have decreased and the purchaser may now be more willing to accept an asset sale.

Corporate Planning and Your Family

It may be possible to reorganize the share structure of your company to permit ownership by your spouse and children should you so desire. Properly planned, a reorganization of the share structure may provide both income splitting and estate planning opportunities. Arranging for share ownership by a spouse and children also could provide for a reduction in tax if the company is sold, particularly if the corporation is a small business corporation, since each family member would be entitled to the $500,000 capital gains exemption.

Reorganizing share capital does have its pitfalls and you should not proceed without proper advice.

As you can see, tax planning for your business may provide opportunities for income splitting, tax deferral, increasing your capital gains exemption, estate planning, and retirement planning. It is clear that attempting to pull all these factors together into a complete and thorough plan is a complex task. Since the presentation here is necessarily restricted, you may wish to consult your professional tax advisor for personalized planning in this area.

9. You and Your Car

The frequent modifications of past years regarding the rules for business use of autos have rendered them complex to the point that they cannot be summarized easily. This chapter highlights the principal tax rules in a way we believe will be of the most value to most readers. Professional advice still will be required to deal adequately with many situations.

TAX ASPECTS FOR EMPLOYEES: EMPLOYEE-PROVIDED AUTOS

Allowances and Reimbursements You Receive

If you own your own car, your company may provide you with various types of benefits in respect of the time you use the car for business or for personal purposes.

One approach is for your employer to pay you an "automobile allowance". This may be calculated to cover only the business-related costs of owning and operating the auto, or may be intended as part of your remuneration package (in excess of business-related costs). Allowances are treated by your employer in one of two ways. If the allowance is not a reasonable amount for business-related purposes, it must be reported on your T4 slip as employment income for the year. In this case, you generally may deduct a portion of the expenses incurred if you operate the auto for business use, provided you are required by contract (not necessarily a written contract) to use the auto in the course of your employment and meet certain other criteria. Details of the available deductions are discussed in the next section.

Alternatively, if the employer pays you for business use, and if the amount is a reasonable allowance for that purpose, generally, such an allowance cannot be reported as taxable income. If it is not, you are not permitted to deduct expenses attributable to the operation of the auto.

An allowance for use of a motor vehicle will be considered "reasonable" only if it is directly related to the number of business kilometres driven in a year and if no reimbursement is received for expenses related to the same use. To make the first condition possible, you may be expected to provide your employer with detailed records regarding business kilometres driven. Secondly, the allowance will still be considered reasonable even if there is a reimbursement for the cost of additional commercial insurance for the car, parking, tolls and ferries, as long as the allowance is determined without reference to these expenses.

In addition, an allowance will be considered "reasonable" only if the rate per kilometre is reasonable. Your employer may deduct for tax purposes allowances limited to specified amounts per kilometre (discussed later in this chapter). Nonetheless, your employer may pay you at a higher rate without reporting it as taxable income to you if the higher rate is "reasonable". However, your employer may not be willing to incur a non-deductible expense. As well, Revenue Canada has stated it considers that, generally, the prescribed rate for the employer's deduction is representative of a reasonable per-kilometre allowance. In any event, you should keep records to indicate the cost of operating your car in case you are called upon to support the allowance.

You may want to consider the alternative of having the allowance treated as taxable remuneration. If this is done, you will be permitted to deduct at least a proportion of the costs of operating the auto for business purposes if you meet all the criteria. In many circumstances, this may work out to your advantage.

Specific reimbursements of direct costs incurred in the operation of your car in your employer's business (e.g., gas and oil related to identifiable business travel) are not allowances and are not considered in calculating your taxable income.

Deducting Expenses from Your Taxable Income

Eligibility. You may be allowed to claim various deductions for the ownership and operating costs of your auto related to its use in the course of your employment. To be eligible for these deductions, you must not be in receipt of a tax-free allowance, and you must be required by your terms of employment (technically your contract of employment, which need not be written) to pay your own travel expenses. You also must be required to work away from the office or in different places on an ordinary basis. A prescribed form (T2200) must be signed by your employer to confirm that these conditions have been met and must be filed with your tax return. If you are claiming expenses, any payment received from your employer in respect of ownership of the car must be a taxable allowance, and any reimbursement of operating expenses by your employer must be subtracted from any deduction claimed in relation to the same expense.

Salesmen selling property or negotiating contracts for their employers, and remunerated by commissions related to the volume of sales made or the contracts negotiated, may deduct auto and other expenses only up to the amount of such commissions, unless travelling expenses are the only type of expenses being claimed.

If you qualify to deduct auto expenses, you may deduct the business proportion of the actual costs of ownership and operation, subject to the limitations discussed below for autos costing more than $24,000 ($20,000 for autos acquired before September 1, 1989).

Deductions for Owned Vehicles

If you own the car you use for business purposes, you are permitted Capital Cost Allowance (CCA) on the total cost including provincial sales tax (PST), but only on a maximum cost of $24,000 (including PST). This applies for all autos acquired on or after September 1, 1989 ($20,000 for autos acquired after June 17, 1987, and before September 1, 1989). If you acquired the car from a non-arm's length person (a related person), the cost for CCA purposes is the least of $24,000, fair market value immediately before the disposition, and the transferor's undepreciated capital cost (UCC) immediately before the transfer.

Upon disposition of an auto, the terminal loss and recapture rules will cease to apply where the cost is in excess of $24,000 ($20,000 for autos acquired after June 17, 1987, and before September 1, 1989).

CCA is allowed at 30 per cent on a declining balance basis and, under the new system, each car in excess of $24,000 will be in a separate pool within a class (class 10.1).

For instance, if the cost of your car purchased on October 1, 1990, is $35,000, because of the half-year rule, applicable in the first year of ownership, you may claim 15 per cent of $24,000 or $3,600, in that year. In the second year you may claim 30 per cent of $20,400 ($24,000 - $3,600), or $6,120; in the third year you may claim $4,284, and so on. In the year in which the car is sold there will be no assets in the class at year end and no CCA can be calculated. However, one-half of the depreciation (CCA) that would have been allowed in the year of sale if the car were still owned at year end will be deductible, provided you acquire another car during the year with a cost in excess of $24,000 and this automobile is held at the end of the year. When a class is exhausted for other types of depreciable assets, any positive balance remaining usually may be written off and any negative balance must be taken into income. This, however, will not apply to cars where the cost is more than the prescribed amount.

The rules are different where the cost of the auto is less than the prescribed amount. In this case, the recapture and terminal loss rules will apply.

You also are permitted to deduct interest on a loan that is directly related to the purchase of the car. The interest deduction is limited to a maximum average of $300 per month ($250 for autos acquired before September 1, 1989) for the period that the loan is outstanding.

The reduced amounts of depreciation and interest calculated as above are further reduced in relation to business versus personal use as discussed in a later section.

Deductions for Leased Vehicles

If you lease your car, you may deduct the least of:

- the actual lease cost; or
- $650 per month ($600 for leases before September 1, 1989); or
- the actual lease cost times $24,000 and divided by 85 per cent of the manufacturer's suggested list price plus provincial sales tax (minimum $28,235 or $23,529 for leases before September 1, 1989). For leases entered into after 1990, no reference will be made to provincial sales tax.

If your car's manufacturer's suggested list price plus provincial sales tax (any dealer can supply it) is $34,000 and the monthly lease payment under a lease entered into on October 1, 1990, is $700, the three alternatives will be $700, $650 and $581 ($700 × $24,000 / 85 per cent of $34,000). The maximum deduction will be $581. (The monthly lease payment for any car will be affected by the length of the lease and the purchase option price on lease expiry, as well as by negotiation. Thus, this example is not necessarily representative of the circumstances that will apply to this price range of car.)

The amount calculated by comparing these three alternatives is also further reduced by the ratio of personal use to total use, as discussed below.

Reductions for Personal Use

Deductible ownership or lease costs as calculated above must be reduced further by multiplying them by the ratio of business kilometres to total kilometres.

Your deduction for operating costs also is limited to the proportion of expenses for fuel, repairs and maintenance that is calculated by multiplying the costs by the ratio of business kilometres to total kilometres travelled. Thus, if you use the car 50 per cent for business, 50 per cent of the expenses are deductible.

Purchase Assistance

Your employer may be willing to assist you in the purchase of your car. This assistance commonly takes the form of an interest-free (or low-interest-rate) loan. In this case, the foregone interest is considered a taxable benefit at government-prescribed rates of interest. Accordingly, your taxable earnings are increased by the amount of the loan outstanding times the prescribed interest rate for the period the loan is outstanding. However, this interest amount is considered to have been paid by you and you may deduct a proportion of the deemed interest payment using the rules discussed above.

Because you probably would have paid more than the prescribed rate if you had borrowed the money from a bank, but the cost to the employer (including lost investment income) is likely to approximate the prescribed rate, such a loan may be one of the best ways of receiving a real benefit at a relatively low tax cost. This would apply whether or not the loan was specifically intended for the purchase of an automobile.

TAX ASPECTS FOR EMPLOYEES: COMPANY-PROVIDED AUTOS

If your company provides you with a car, you could be required to include several amounts in taxable income. These amounts include a standby charge (a notional charge for generally making the car available to you), any benefit you receive for operating expenses paid by your employer for personal use, and taxable allowances. Specific reimbursement of out-of-pocket expenses such as gasoline and parking directly related to business use would not be included as a taxable benefit. Generally, your employer will report the taxable amounts on your T4. However, it is to your advantage to understand how they are calculated. In some cases (and assuming you have a choice), you may prefer to own your own vehicle and receive an allowance, rather than using a car provided by your employer.

Standby Charge

You must include in your taxable income a "standby charge", which is designed as a rough measure of the benefit to you of having the car available for personal use. This charge is calculated differently depending on whether the car is owned or leased by your employer.

Owned Vehicles. If the auto is owned by your employer, the standby charge is 2 per cent of the original cost of the car (including provincial sales tax) for each month the car is available to you (24 per cent for a full year). This 2 per cent is calculated on the full cost of the car, regardless of whether this cost is in excess of $24,000.

This standby charge may be reduced where you use the car all or substantially all for business (interpreted by Revenue Canada as 90 per cent or more) and your personal use is under 1,000 kilometres per month. In this case, basically the standby charge is calculated as follows:

$$\text{Standby charge otherwise calculated} \times \frac{\text{kilometres for personal use in the year}}{1{,}000 \times \text{number of months in the year in which the car is available to the employee}}$$

For instance, if your personal use is only 200 kilometres per month and this equals 5 per cent of the total use, you will be taxable on only 20 per cent (2,400 km/12,000 km) of the standby charge otherwise calculated. You should note, however, that commuting to your employer's office is considered personal (not business) use of the car.

In those situations where a car is available to you only for business use, such as a pooled car arrangement or a company limousine, this rule means you will not have to include any amount in income in respect of a standby charge. On the other hand, you should realize that if you live 10 kilometres from work and drive that car to and from the office every day, but do not otherwise use it for personal purposes, you still would drive roughly 4,500 personal kilometres a year. To qualify for any reduction in the standby charge, your total use would have to exceed 45,000 kilometres. If you lived 20 kilometres from work, you would have to clock up a total of 90,000 business kilometres a year.

An optional method is available for calculating the standby charge if you are employed principally in selling new or used cars.

The standby rules apply to members of a partnership as if they were employees.

Leased Vehicles. The standby charge included in your income for autos leased by your employer is two-thirds of the lease cost including sales tax and any amount included in the lease cost for repairs and maintenance, but excluding any amount included for insurance. (You should note that the insurance amount is included in operating costs for the purpose of determining any operating benefit.) This charge is calculated on the full lease cost paid by your employer, whether or not the amount in respect of which your employer may claim deductions is the full cost.

It may be better for you if your employer leases the car rather than owns it. Two-thirds of the lease payment may work out to less than 24 per cent of the cost that would be chargeable if the employer owned the vehicle (you need to have a specific lease versus purchase quote to know). And, there is greater flexibility in that some service costs can be included in the lease contract and hence be taxable benefits to you only to the extent of two-thirds.

Where your personal use is less than 10 per cent and less than 1,000 kilometres per month, this standby charge also may be reduced as discussed under owned vehicles above.

Reimbursements to Your Employer

If you reimburse your employer for part of the cost of the auto, the standby charge otherwise included in your income is reduced by the amount of your reimbursement to your employer. This offers you an advantage where the employer leases the car because you deduct your full lease payment against an amount that is only two-thirds of the lease cost. In the case of a lease, however, the reimbursement is taxed punitively to your employer as discussed further below. Therefore, he may be reluctant to permit such an arrangement.

Other Ownership and Operating Expenses

If your employer also pays for such items as insurance, licence, fuel, and repairs and maintenance, you may have an additional taxable benefit. This benefit is measured by the amount of costs paid by the employer times the ratio of personal to total kilometres driven less any reimbursements you make to your employer.

You may not claim deductions on your tax return for operating expenses that have been reimbursed by your employer and excluded from taxable income.

Election in Respect of Operating Expenses

If you use the car primarily for business, you may elect to include as taxable income in respect of operating expenses paid by your employer an amount equal to one-half of the standby charge. This is an alternative to the amount included based on actual costs paid by the employer. Revenue Canada has suggested informally that for this purpose "primarily" means at least 50 per cent. If you elect to use this method, you must notify your employer in writing before the end of the applicable year that you are making the election.

Other Incidental Personal Costs

Amounts paid by your employer for other incidental personal costs, such as non-business parking expenses, are included in your income as a taxable benefit.

Shareholders

The same rules with respect to employee automobile benefits generally apply to a shareholder of a corporation.

TAX ASPECTS FOR EMPLOYERS AND SELF-EMPLOYED INDIVIDUALS

Allowances

A reasonable allowance paid to an employee for business purposes and based on the number of business kilometres driven in the year is not included in the employee's income. To lessen the administrative difficulty of maintaining mileage records for each employee on a regular basis, Revenue Canada will allow a tax-free fixed allowance to be paid to an employee during the year provided the following conditions exist:

- There is a pre-established per-kilometre rate.
- The rate and the advance are reasonable.
- At the earlier of the calendar year end or when the employee ceases to be employed, the actual kilometres travelled for business purposes are calculated. If the employer has overpaid, the employee must refund the excess to the employer. If the employee was underpaid, the employer will make up the difference.

- The employee is not required to include the amount in income under any other provision of the Income Tax Act.

Deductible Expenditures

If your employees use their own cars for business you may deduct certain allowances or reimbursements you pay them in respect of the business use.

If you provide cars to your employees, you need to be aware of the rules regarding available deductions for these expenditures. Generally, your deductible amounts are limited to non-capital, "reasonable" expenses incurred for the purpose of earning income from a business, profession, or property.

Accordingly, you may deduct all leasing or ownership costs up to the luxury car limitations mentioned above, and reasonable operating costs, parking costs, and so forth for the autos provided. You also may deduct interest expense incurred on debt used directly to purchase the autos up to a maximum of $300 ($250 for autos acquired after June 17, 1987, and before September 1, 1989) per month per car, for the period the loans are outstanding.

Employer Deductions in Respect of Employee-Provided Autos

As an employer, you can deduct certain distance-based car allowances paid to an employee in respect of the use of his or her car for the benefit of your business, even when these are not reported as taxable income of the employee. You may deduct fully any car allowances or similar payments that are reported on the employee's T4 as fully taxable.

You will be permitted to deduct tax-free allowances to an employee to the extent that they do not exceed 31 cents for each of the first 5,000 business kilometres driven by the employee in a year, and 25 cents for each additional business kilometre. An additional four cents per kilometre is allowed in the Yukon and the Northwest Territories.

You may deduct payments made regarding fuel, maintenance, and repairs in full, although the part of these costs related to personal use of the car will be taxable income to the employee.

Employer Deductions in Respect of Company-Provided Autos

If your company purchases or leases autos that are provided to employees, you will be required to calculate a standby charge, as discussed above, and include the taxable benefit on your employees' T4s.

Company-Owned Cars

You will be permitted regular CCA (Capital Cost Allowance) deductions for autos you own that are used in business. Existing CCA rules apply to autos costing $24,000 or less, including PST. The autos will be included in the current CCA class 10, which allows a 30 per cent CCA rate. Current recapture and terminal loss and pooling rules continue to apply for cars meeting the criteria described above.

If you purchase a car costing in excess of $24,000, each car must be placed in a separate, new, CCA class 10.1. The other tax measures for employees described above in the section entitled "Deductions for Owned Vehicles" also apply to employers.

Leased Cars

If the company provides leased autos to its employees, the maximum deduction regarding the lease cost is the same as the deduction available to individuals, which was described before. Additional tax rules exist to prevent refundable amounts paid to the lessor from reducing the monthly amount of rent and indirectly increasing the maximum allowable deduction.

You should note that if you provide your employees with leased autos, any reimbursement by an employee of your lease expense will reduce the deductible portion of your cost. This can have a very punitive effect in the case of luxury cars. For instance, if you pay $1,800 per month for the lease entered into on October 1, 1990, your maximum deduction before any reimbursement may be $650. If the employee reimbursement is $650 or greater, you obtain no deduction. If the reimbursement is less than $650, it must be deducted from the $650 allowable deduction.

PLANNING FOR BUSINESS USE OF AUTOMOBILES

As you can see, the rules are very complex. As a result, in most cases, specific review of existing policies and of available alternatives is necessary to maximize the tax deductions and the benefits to employees.

The result of such analysis may be to show that you should think about different approaches. For instance, perhaps you should:

- consider an interest-free loan instead of a car allowance or a company car;
- consider having the employer provide a leased car over a purchased car;
- lease the car initially and purchase it at a later date; or
- consider having a car available to you that is used exclusively for business, or at least 90 per cent.

You should consult your professional advisor to see whether particular approaches can result in significant savings over the costs that might otherwise be incurred.

Gasoline Excise Tax

The price of gasoline includes a federal Excise Tax of 8.5 cents per litre for unleaded gas and 9.5 cents for leaded gas. Until December 31, 1990, you may qualify for a refund of this tax of 1.5 cents per litre where its cost is deductible for income tax purposes. An information bulletin on persons and expenditures eligible for the refund and the required application form (Form XE-8) are available from any Customs and Excise Taxation Office or Post Office. Note that the amount of the refund must be included in income or the amount of gasoline expenses reduced.

10. Estate Planning

You might be inclined to skip this chapter, in the mistaken belief that you are either not old enough or not rich enough to have an "estate" that is worth planning. The fact is that virtually everyone over the age of majority should give some thought to what will happen to his or her assets in the event of death, and to make arrangements so that family members who are financially dependent on them are adequately provided for.

Each year, thousands of Canadians die in accidents. A large number of these unfortunate souls die without even having a will. Although the odds are that you will live to a ripe old age, you owe it to yourself, and to your family, to "put your house in order".

Your estate plan can be as simple, or as complex, as you want it to be. However, your personal and financial circumstances will dictate, to some extent, the degree of complexity. For example, if you are a business owner, your estate plan should reflect arrangements for the succession of ownership to your offspring, or for a sale of the business to outsiders. This will be discussed in more detail later in this chapter.

Estate planning is the ongoing process of creating and maintaining a program designed to preserve your accumulated wealth and ensure its most effective and beneficial distribution to succeeding generations, according to your wishes.

Several developments in recent years have affected virtually all estate plans and those who are contemplating an estate planning program:

- The lifetime capital gains exemption can alter the way in which assets are passed on to succeeding generations.
- The constant tightening up of the rules preventing income splitting among family members can necessitate the restructuring of many estate planning approaches.
- The alternative minimum tax (AMT) can affect a number of upper income Canadians, particularly those with "tax shelter" type investments.
- New or revised family law acts in several provinces have a great impact on the transfer of assets from one generation to the next.

OBJECTIVES

In general, the objectives of estate planning are to:

- ensure that you and your family are provided for adequately now and in the future (i.e., during your retirement), and that your heirs are adequately provided for after your death;
- distribute assets according to your wishes, both during your lifetime and on your death, while ensuring that the maximum benefits available accrue to your beneficiaries;
- minimize various forms of wealth erosion, taxes being the most prominent, both now and in the future.

Your estate planning objectives should be realistic. More importantly, your estate plan should be reviewed frequently and be flexible enough to accommodate unexpected changes in your financial or personal situation, as well as changes beyond your control, such as new legislative developments.

Financial Considerations

The first step in developing an estate plan is to determine where you stand today in terms of assets, liabilities, and income. You should also try to project the future direction of your affairs, including possible inheritances, asset liquidations such as sale of a business or property, paying off mortgages, education costs for children, acquiring a recreation or retirement property, and so on. At the same time, you should attempt to assess how the economy's performance might affect your assets and income in the future. Using the "rule of 72", if inflation averages 6 per cent a year, one dollar today will be worth 50 cents in today's dollars in approximately 12 years (72 divided by 6). In 24 years, that dollar will be worth only about 25 cents.

Estate Planning Advisor's Requirements

Above all, a professional estate planner needs accurate and up-to-date information concerning your financial affairs, as well as a clear understanding of your financial and personal objectives. He or she must be as well informed about your financial affairs as you are. Remember that your estate plan is only as good as the information that goes into its development.

An effective estate plan requires the cooperation and input of a number of individuals, including your accountant, lawyer, insurance agent, financial advisor, and to some extent your business associates. It is also recommended that you involve your spouse in setting your estate planning objectives. If your affairs are the least bit complicated and your spouse is expected to manage them on your death, involving him or her now makes good sense. However, this may not suit everyone.

Tax Planning Objectives

From a tax point of view, your estate planning objectives can be summarized as follows:

- minimize and defer taxes now and in the future, to preserve your accumulated wealth;
- shift any potential tax burden associated with a particular asset to your heirs so that taxes become payable only when your heirs eventually sell the asset;

- minimize taxes at death so that as much as possible of your accumulated wealth passes to your heirs.

YOUR CHANGING ESTATE PLAN

To assist you in formulating your own estate planning objectives, the following is a summary of the type of estate planning considerations that a typical family might contemplate throughout the years. You will notice that their concerns vary with the changing requirements and circumstances of the family. But remember, this is just a theoretical example of the types of estate planning concerns you may encounter. Your own estate plan will depend on the particular circumstances of you and your family.

Estate Planning Early in Life

During the period from your mid-twenties to about age 40, it is likely that you will get married and start a family, will have little in the way of substantial assets, and will be establishing yourself in your career or business. In this case, your goal is to protect your dependants in the event that you or your spouse die or become otherwise unable to provide for them. Your estate plan may extend no further than paying down the mortgage on the family home and ensuring that you have sufficient life insurance (likely term insurance) and long-term disability insurance in place. It is likely that your will would leave all your assets outright to your spouse.

Once you have more income to devote to estate planning, you will likely want to start saving for future acquisitions, for your children's education, and for your retirement. You will likely contribute to registered retirement savings plans (RRSPs) for both yourself and your spouse. At some point, you may find it advantageous to pay higher premiums to obtain the added security and investment benefits available with permanent life insurance.

Planning in Middle Age

From your forties to your mid-fifties, you may well have more substantial assets and be enjoying a larger income. However, you may also be facing increased expenditures such as post-secondary education for your children. During this period, you will continue contributing to a retirement plan, whether an RRSP or a registered pension plan. You may feel you can discontinue your term life insurance policy, while continuing with coverage under a permanent policy. This may also be a good time to restructure your business affairs and investments to reduce current taxes and facilitate the accumulation of savings and other assets for your retirement.

Planning for Retirement

Once you have reached your mid-fifties, it is time to give serious consideration to planning for your retirement. You must ensure that you will have sufficient retirement income to cover your needs and savings to cover unforeseen events. You will likely continue with contributions to your RRSPs or pension plan, and you will probably continue to make additional investments. You might want to determine what type of retirement income will best suit your needs once your RRSPs and pension plans have matured. If you have a business, you may wish to sell it to further supplement your retirement income, or to pass the management of it to others.

It is also time to consider how you wish to dispose of your assets upon your death. The deemed disposition rules in the Income Tax Act impose a tax on unrealized capital gains at the time of your death, which could seriously erode the value of your assets, particularly if your lifetime capital gains exemption has been fully used up during your lifetime. However, by careful disposition of your assets during your lifetime and with a carefully drafted will, you may be able to minimize the tax consequences of the deemed disposition rules. You may want to consider gifting some of your assets to your heirs during your lifetime, or establishing trusts for their benefit to take effect either during your lifetime or after your death.

YOUR WILL

Your will and your spouse's are the most important elements in your testamentary estate planning (i.e., estate planning after your death). In your will, you appoint the executor(s) of your estate, name your beneficiaries and provide for the distribution of your assets according to your wishes. It is important that you consult your spouse in the preparation of your will so that the spouse understands the reasons for the provisions that are included. If your spouse agrees with the terms of the will, he or she will be less likely to use family law rules to attack the will after your death.

The Executor

The role of the executor (and trustee) under a will involves onerous responsibilities. You should consider not only the willingness of the person to serve, but also his or her appropriateness for the position. Two of the major criteria are the familiarity of the person with your affairs and the technical competence required to manage your affairs.

The executor is charged with interpreting your wishes as expressed in your will and in other documents, and carrying them out to the best of his or her ability. He or she should be empowered by the provisions of your will to make virtually all decisions concerning your estate that you have not anticipated.

Most importantly, your executor is charged with maintaining the value of your estate until assets are distributed to the beneficiaries. Thus, if he or she feels your business would benefit from outside management help before your beneficiaries take it over, your will must empower him or her to do so. If this is not the case and your spouse or your children are incapable of managing the business once they gain control, there is little the executor can do but advise them to bring in outside expertise, or perhaps advise them to sell the business before its value seriously declines.

Bear in mind that a great deal of what happens after your death depends on the arrangements you have made before you die, particularly in your will. If your instructions are not specific enough, your executor, although acting in good faith, may misinterpret your wishes or may see his or her powers contested in court.

Dying Intestate

It is a commonly held belief that, in the absence of a will, a surviving spouse will automatically inherit the entire estate of the deceased. In fact, when a person dies intestate (i.e., without a will or without a validly drafted and executed will), or partially intestate (i.e., with a will that does not provide for the disposition of all his or her property), the distribution of the property not covered by a will is decided on his or her behalf by provincial law relating to intestate succession and family law.

Such law varies from province to province. For example, the law in several provinces provides that if a person dies without a will, the spouse receives the first $75,000 of the estate and shares the balance with the children, if any. Since this type of distribution is arbitrary, it will not in most circumstances satisfy the wishes of the deceased and the needs of individual family members. In Quebec, if a person dies without a will, one-third of the estate is transferred to the surviving spouse and two-thirds is transferred to the children.

Reviewing Your Will

A good rule of thumb is that your will should be reviewed, and revised if necessary, at least every five years. Your will should be revised immediately in the event of the death of an intended beneficiary or the executor, or because of changes in your family situation or financial circumstances.

Changes in the law may also affect the validity of your will. For instance, in some provinces legislation respecting division of matrimonial property will override the provisions of your will. Furthermore, legislation in most provinces (not including Quebec) provides that you may not totally disinherit your spouse or a dependant. And it is not just your will that must be periodically reviewed. Do not forget other parts of your estate plan such as insurance policies, retirement savings and pension plans. You must remember to change beneficiary designations or a substantial part of your estate may go to someone you no longer wish to benefit.

Remember that a properly drafted will requires special expertise. To avoid pitfalls and difficulties in the future, professional legal advice should be sought in all cases from lawyers experienced in wills and family law. It is also advisable to have your tax advisor review the will prior to signing it.

TAXATION ON DEATH

If you understand how taxation applies on death, you should be better equipped to decide how to effectively provide for the distribution of your assets in your will and possibly how to distribute assets during your lifetime.

There are no Canadian death taxes, federal or provincial, levied on the value of the assets that pass to beneficiaries. Only income amounts received or deemed to be received by the deceased, and capital gains realized (or deemed to be realized), are subject to tax.

On death, four distinct taxpaying entities may result:

- the deceased, whose income from January 1 to the date of death is taxed in a terminal tax return and, in the case of certain income, in a separate tax return;
- the estate, as long as it has not been settled by the executor;
- any ongoing trusts created under the deceased's will;
- the beneficiaries.

Deemed Disposition Rules

In the year of death, an individual's taxation year runs from January 1 to the date of death. A final return of income, the "terminal return", is required to be filed. All income earned to the date of death must be reported. This includes interest, rents, royalties, annuities, remuneration from employment, and other amounts payable on a periodic basis that were accrued but not due at the time of death, as well as amounts due but not paid. Also included are net taxable capital gains or losses realized prior to death and not included in income in a previous year.

In addition, the deceased is deemed to have disposed of all capital property immediately before death. Non-depreciable capital property is deemed disposed of at its fair market value immediately before death. Depreciable capital property is deemed disposed of at a value midway between its undepreciated capital cost and its fair market value. These deemed dispositions can result in capital gains and losses, as well as a terminal loss or recapture of depreciation already claimed, which must be included in the terminal return.

Resource properties are defined in the Act to be something other than capital property. A deemed disposition of a resource property at death results in the inclusion of the full fair market value as income on the terminal return.

In other words, even though there has not been an actual sale of the property, the deceased is taxed as though all his or her property had been sold just prior to death. If capital assets have appreciated significantly from the time of their acquisition, or resource properties have a significant fair market value, a large tax assessment on the "profit" from these deemed dispositions may result. Since there has been no actual sale of assets, the estate may have difficulty paying any taxes that are levied. It should be noted that the alternative minimum tax (AMT) is not applicable in the year of death.

Any unused capital gain exemption may be claimed to reduce capital gains resulting from deemed dispositions.

An individual may avoid some of the adverse tax consequences of the deemed disposition rules in two specific situations:

- If property of any kind is transferred to a spouse or spousal trust, no capital gains, recapture of depreciation, etc. arise on death, unless elected otherwise, and the spouse or spousal trust inherits the deceased's tax cost (i.e., the cost at which the deceased acquired or was deemed to have acquired the property). However, it should be ensured that the deceased has fully used his or her lifetime capital gains exemption before using this method of relieving taxes and that assets are transferred to a spouse or spousal trust at cost. When a principal residence is transferred to a spouse or spousal trust, the spouse or spousal trust retains the deceased's principal residence exemption. Any accrued gain on a principal residence remains tax-free and is not included under the lifetime capital gains exemption. (See Chapter 7.)

- If farm property, an interest in a family farm partnership, or shares in a family farm corporation are bequeathed to a child, grandchild, or great-grandchild of the deceased, there is a complete tax deferral on the transfer and the child assumes the deceased's tax cost. However, make sure that the lifetime capital gains exemption of the deceased has been fully used up, either before or on death, as this increases the tax cost of the farm property for the child.

These situations, involving deferral of taxes that might otherwise be payable due to the deemed disposition rules, are commonly known as "rollovers". Your heirs assume any potential tax liability, which will be payable only when they dispose of or are deemed to dispose of the property.

Optional Tax Returns

If the deceased was the proprietor of or a partner in a business, was a beneficiary of a testamentary trust, or had earned "rights or things" (which are generally unrealized income amounts at the date of death), the executor of the estate may have the option of reporting some of the business, trust, or "rights or things" income on three additional separate returns.

The advantage in filing these separate returns is that each return treats the deceased as a separate person. Full personal tax credits are permitted on each return, which can produce a tax saving, and the splitting of income among the different returns produces a further saving because of the graduated tax rate system.

Taxation of the Estate

Frequently, income-producing assets are held by the estate in trust before passing to specific beneficiaries. Generally, all income earned and received by the estate from the date of death is taxed in the estate, except for income payable or distributed to beneficiaries, or elected to be attributed to a preferred beneficiary, in which cases it is taxed in the hands of the beneficiaries.

Your will should be drafted to empower the executor of your estate to undertake some testamentary tax planning that can reduce taxes in your terminal return and reduce the impact of taxes on your beneficiaries.

Foreign Death Taxes

If you have any assets located in the United States, or if you or any of your beneficiaries is a citizen or resident of the United States, U.S. federal estate tax and state inheritance taxes may apply. Over the last few years, the U.S. estate tax rates were drastically increased, with the result that thousands of Canadian residents who own property in the United States face a large U.S. estate tax on death. If you own U.S. assets, you should consult with your tax advisor to determine what steps, if any, might be taken to reduce or eliminate the U.S. estate tax exposure.

Many other countries levy estate taxes in some form. If you may be subject to these taxes, obtaining professional advice is recommended.

TOOLS AND PLANNING TECHNIQUES

There is often a "cost" involved in implementing some of the estate planning strategies outlined below. A tax saving could be accompanied by loss of control over the related asset or perhaps the overall flexibility of your estate plan might be impaired to some extent. The tools and techniques that you might use depend on your personal and financial situation and your estate planning objectives.

Gifting

The most direct method of accomplishing a number of the more common estate planning goals is to gift assets to your potential heirs during your lifetime. Since ownership is transferred, the future capital appreciation of the assets and the related future tax liability are also transferred. However, there are three drawbacks to gifting.

First, if the asset is transferred to your spouse or a related child under the age of 18, you will be subject to "attribution rules". These provide that if you gift any type of asset to your spouse or a related child under 18 years of age, by any means whatsoever, either directly or indirectly, any income, which includes interest, dividend, and rental income, earned on the property is taxed in your hands until the marriage breaks down or until the year the child turns 18. Also, if your spouse realizes capital gains or losses on the sale of such transferred property, you must recognize the gain or loss for tax purposes. The attribution of capital gains and losses does not apply in respect of transfers to minor children. The attribution rules have been considerably expanded in scope in recent years. (See Chapter 4.)

Second, since ownership of the asset is transferred, you lose control over the asset and you no longer have access to its future income-earning capability.

Third, when you gift an asset to any person, except your spouse, during your lifetime, you generally are deemed to have received proceeds of disposition equal to the fair market value of the asset at that time and you must immediately recognize for tax purposes any resulting capital gain or loss. In other words, you would be taxed as though you received proceeds equal to the fair market value of the asset, even though it may have been a gift or was transferred for a nominal amount. Such a gain is nonetheless eligible for your lifetime capital gains exemption.

As in the case of deemed dispositions that occur on death, there are certain exceptions to the above deemed disposition inter vivos rule. You may be able to defer the tax via a rollover when:

- property is transferred to a spouse or a spousal trust (although future capital gains and losses will be attributed back to you);
- farm property is transferred to a child, grandchild or great-grandchild.

It is more beneficial to claim any gain under your $100,000 lifetime capital gains exemption if you do not otherwise expect to fully use it, before opting to use the rollovers, which simply defer tax to future years.

If you are a shareholder of a Canadian private corporation which uses all or substantially all of the fair market value of its assets in carrying on an active business primarily in Canada, or own qualified farm property, you may also be eligible for a special $400,000 lifetime capital gains exemption on the disposition of shares of the company. (See Chapter 7.) If you have not already used up your special $400,000 exemption, you may want to gift enough of your shares in the company to your children, to trigger a $400,000 capital gain and thereby utilize the exemption. However, this strategy may not make sense if you are planning to sell the company to outsiders. It might be better to save the exemption for the arm's length sale, rather than use it for a "paper transaction" between family members.

Income Splitting

The prime objective of income splitting is to have income that normally would be taxed in your hands at a high tax rate, taxed in the hands of a relative, usually your spouse or child, at a lower tax rate. A detailed examination of income splitting and its effects is contained in Chapter 4.

The Use of Trusts

In its simplest form, a trust merely involves the holding of property by one person for the benefit of another person. In more technical terms, a trust is created when a "settlor" transfers property to a "trustee" who holds the property for the benefit of a "beneficiary". A trust may be either "testamentary" (i.e., arising upon your death) or "inter vivos" (i.e., arising during your lifetime).

A trust can be a useful and flexible device in that it allows you to transfer ownership of an asset to an intended heir, while you, or actually the trustee of the trust, are able to maintain control over the asset. It permits you to accomplish a number of your estate planning goals. Trusts may be used for such varied purposes as funding a child's education, providing for handicapped children or obtaining professional property management.

To achieve a tax saving, you must first relinquish ownership of the assets held by the trust, although in some cases you may still control the management and operation of the trust itself, and, secondly, you must avoid the attribution rules. (See Chapter 4.)

Income earned and left in a trust is taxed as if the trust were a separate individual taxpayer, although some special rules apply (e.g., trusts cannot claim personal tax credits). An inter vivos trust is taxed at the top personal rate. Testamentary trusts are taxed more favourably at the progressive tax rates applied to individuals.

However, if trust income is distributed to a beneficiary, whether directly by means of an actual distribution or by means of the preferred beneficiary election (see below), or is distributable, such amounts are deducted from trust income and taxed in the hands of the beneficiary, assuming the attribution rules do not apply. This can result in some tax savings if the beneficiary is taxed at a lower marginal rate.

The Income Tax Act provides that certain forms of income earned in a trust retain their character when distributed to beneficiaries and taxed in their hands. For example, eligible Canadian taxable dividends received by a trust and distributed to a beneficiary are eligible for the dividend tax credit. Capital gains retain their identity and are eligible for the beneficiary's lifetime capital gains exemption, if they are so designated by the trust.

Preferred Beneficiary Election. By making this election, income earned by the trust is taxed in the hands of the beneficiary, even though the income remains in the trust. A preferred beneficiary must be a Canadian resident and one of the following:

- the settlor of the trust, or his or her spouse or former spouse;
- a child, grandchild, or great-grandchild of the settlor;
- the spouse (but not former spouse) of a child, grandchild, or great grandchild of the settlor.

In addition, the settlor must contribute more to the trust than any other taxpayer.

Deemed Disposition Rule for Trusts. Special rules prevent trusts from holding property for an indefinite period, thereby deferring the inclusion of capital gains in income for tax purposes. The general rule provides for a deemed disposition by a trust of all its capital property every 21 years for notional proceeds of sale equal to the fair market value of the property. The main exception to this rule applies to certain spousal trusts that are deemed to dispose of their property on the death of the surviving spouse.

Estate Freezing

An estate freeze can be defined in general terms as a method of organizing your affairs so as to permit any future appreciation in the value of selected assets to accrue to others, usually your children.

Gifting capital property to a child should be differentiated from estate freezing. If assets are gifted to a child, no value is received in return and control is lost. Under an estate freeze, you retain, or at least have access to, the current value of the frozen assets; only the future increases in value are transferred to the child. It is also possible for you to retain control over those assets. Unlike estate freezing, gifting assets to your child eliminates tax on your death, but it also may result in an immediate tax liability and probably achieves none of your other estate planning goals.

Direct Sale. Selling an asset to your child, the simplest of estate freezes, may achieve some or even all the goals. Tax is eliminated on death, but you must include any capital gain in income for tax purposes in the year of sale. Such a gain is eligible for your lifetime capital gains exemption. Normally, you would take back a note payable from the child as payment of the sale price. Thus you can dispose of a growth asset and obtain a fixed value asset in its place. Interest does not have to be payable on the note; however, if this is the case, the attribution rules will apply. It is also questionable whether you can legally sell an asset to a minor. You can claim a reserve (i.e., not recognize the full capital gain) if you have not received all proceeds from the sale and the unpaid proceeds are not yet due (for example, they are represented by a demand note that is payable sometime after demand for payment is made). Thus, you might claim a reserve in respect of any portion of the gain not covered by your lifetime exemption. (See Chapter 7.) The taxable capital gain must be brought into your income over, at most, the succeeding four or nine years, depending on the type of asset sold. When the reserve amount is included in income, it is eligible for the lifetime capital gains exemption, provided the related property was disposed of after 1984.

The fact that you are able to demand partial or full payment on the note at any time may or may not represent some form of control over the asset. Transferring the asset to a trust of which the child is a beneficiary may permit you to exercise more control over the asset.

Corporate Freeze. Most individuals are concerned with freezing assets that are likely to increase substantially in value in the future. The most common are business assets, usually in the form of shares of a private corporation controlled by the individual. Using a corporation in an estate freeze provides the individual with considerable flexibility and, if properly structured, enables him or her to achieve each of the estate freezing goals mentioned above.

Taking Advantage of Tax Provisions

Principal Residence Exemption. Detailed rules on the principal residence exemption are contained in Chapter 2. A number of estate planning options involve changes in the ownership of a principal residence.

If two residences are currently owned by a married couple (e.g., a city home and a summer cottage) and both expect to fully use their lifetime capital gains exemptions, consideration might be given to transferring ownership of one property, say the cottage, to children or grandchildren who reside in the residence for at least part of the year. This may involve a slight cost currently, i.e., tax on the capital gain from the property appreciating since 1981, but this gain may be covered by the lifetime capital gains exemption. Any future gain realized on the disposition of the other property retained by the couple would generally be tax-free under the principal residence rules. As well, since the attribution rules do not apply to capital gains realized on property that was transferred to children, whether or not they are under 18, any capital gain realized when the cottage is subsequently sold would be taxable in the hands of the children. Alternatively, the cottage could be designated as the principal residence of a child or children and thus full exemption would apply.

Of course, if you sell or gift the cottage directly to the children, you and your spouse no longer have any legal right to occupy it. Taking back a demand note payable on the sale may give you some control over the property, but perhaps not enough to suit your wishes. One solution might be to give the property to a discretionary trust for you and your children. The trust agreement might be structured to permit you to give the cottage to a particular child at some time in the future, while ensuring that the future increase in value accrues to the ultimate owner.

Registered Retirement Savings Plans (RRSPs). RRSPs are probably the most common tax deferral vehicles in use today. Stated simply, the immediate tax benefit of an RRSP is that it reduces annual income for tax purposes (within specified limits) by the amount of the annual contribution and shelters the income accumulating in the plan from taxation. As well, an RRSP will provide you with a fund that, on your death, might be passed on to your spouse who is subject to a lower tax rate and, in certain circumstances, to your children. (See Chapter 6.)

Registered Pension Plans. Contributions to your registered pension plan have the immediate tax benefit of reducing your taxable income by the amount of that contribution and sheltering the income accumulating in the plan from taxation. Membership in such a plan reduces, or may even eliminate, the amount you may contribute each year to an RRSP. Thus, you should carefully consider the relative merits of each plan to determine which will be of the most benefit to you, assuming that you can opt out of your employer's registered pension plan.

Spouse and Spousal Trust Rollovers. If you bequeath capital property directly to your spouse or a qualifying spousal trust, the property can be rolled over (i.e., transferred) at your tax cost with no resulting taxation at the time of your death. In order for these spousal rollover rules to apply, certain criteria must be met:

- You must have been resident in Canada immediately before death.
- The ownership of the property must actually be transferred to your spouse or a qualifying spousal trust.
- If the transfer is to your spouse, he or she must have been resident in Canada immediately prior to your death.
- The spousal trust must be testamentary (i.e., one created by your will). It must be resident in Canada when the property vests in the trust.
- Vesting in the spouse or spousal trust generally must occur within 36 months of your death.
- If the property is transferred to a spousal trust, your spouse must be entitled to receive all the income during his or her lifetime and no other person may receive or have the use of any income or capital during that period.

A certain amount of planning can be undertaken after death by your estate's executor. For example, he or she may elect that the rollover provisions not apply to selected assets. This may allow the full use of your lifetime capital gains exemption and of losses carried forward, both of which will reduce the future tax liability of your spouse.

Spousal Rollover of Reserves. With one exception, no reserves can be claimed in the terminal return. The full amount of any reserve outstanding (i.e., claimed by the deceased in a prior year) is added to income in the year of death. The one exception occurs where a qualifying spouse, or spousal trust, inherits the debt that gave rise to the deduction of the reserve. Providing the deceased was resident in Canada immediately before death and the executor and the spouse or spousal trust jointly elect, a deduction for such reserves can be claimed in the terminal return of the deceased. The reserve then flows through to the spouse, or spousal trust, who ultimately pays tax on the income deferred.

The amount of the allowable reserve and the length of time from the date of sale within which proceeds of disposition must be included in income depend on the type of property that was disposed. Capital gains must be included in income over five years, while income from property sold in the ordinary course of business may be recognized over a maximum of four years. Capital gains arising from the transfer of farm assets and shares of eligible small business corporations to a child may be spread over ten years.

Life Insurance

Life insurance plays an important role in estate planning. It can be used for a variety of purposes:

- to provide a base for generating investment income to replace earnings;
- as a tax-sheltered investment vehicle, if properly structured, for the accumulation of funds during your lifetime, with a tax-free payout arising on your death;
- to help the surviving shareholder of a closely held company finance the purchase of shares from the estate or heirs of a deceased shareholder;
- to provide liquidity on death to cover the payment of income taxes, and other debts and expenses;
- to provide additional assets to bequeath to a child or children who is/are not involved in a family business. In the absence of the insurance funds, the non-involved children might receive shares of the family business and be in a position to create problems for those running the business.

Insurance proceeds that are payable as a result of the death of the insured are not subject to income tax in the hands of the beneficiary.

Your financial situation and the future needs of your family will dictate the type and quantity of life insurance you should have. While your insurance agent can provide you with details of a wide variety of individual policies available, you might bear in mind that there are two basic types of life insurance: term policies and permanent policies.

The term policy is generally less expensive at a younger age but has a number of disadvantages. For example, you receive no benefits if the policy is cancelled either by the insurer or yourself. There is usually no obligation for an insurer to continue coverage and the policy will likely not be renewed beyond a certain age. Of course, insurance companies now offer many variations of the term policy that have additional features, such as options that guarantee your insurability to almost any age.

While a permanent policy (often referred to as a "whole life" or "universal" policy) initially involves higher premiums, it has the advantage of also serving as an investment vehicle for you. For example, you may usually borrow against your insurance savings at a favourable rate, and you may receive a lump sum if you decide to cash in the policy at a future date. Most permanent policies are structured so that accruing income is not taxed annually; however, borrowing against the cash surrender value or "cashing in" the policy could result in tax.

Insurance arrangements involving the purchase of a deceased shareholder's shares by the surviving shareholders are more complex and require careful planning.

SUCCESSION AND ESTATE PLANNING FOR BUSINESS ASSETS

If you have an interest in a business, it is likely your largest source of income and you may be expecting the business to provide you with a retirement income. You may also foresee eventually passing control of it to your children. On the other hand, you may wish to sell the business to a partner or third party on your retirement, or arrange for professional management while ownership remains with your family. Whatever your goals, you should know a number of planning techniques that can result in substantial tax savings for you and your family.

Most financial planning, including tax and succession planning, is facilitated if the business is incorporated. If your business is not incorporated, but can be, you should discuss the situation with your professional advisor.

Before examining the planning techniques best suited to you, there are a number of considerations you should address. These include the ability of your spouse or children to manage the business, their relative participation in control and ownership, the time frame for transfer of control, the role of key employees, and your own financial needs after retirement.

The remainder of this chapter examines three major succession and estate planning techniques that focus on business assets:

- exemption of the tax on capital gains on the transfer of shares of an eligible small business corporation and deferral and/or exemption of tax on capital gains on the transfer of eligible farm property to your children;
- methods of corporate estate freezing so that the tax consequences of all or part of future growth in the business are passed to your heirs;
- the use of insurance to fund certain succession planning transactions.

Exemption of Tax on Capital Gains on Shares of Small Business Corporations

The deemed disposition rules consider shares to be disposed of for proceeds equal to fair market value immediately before death. As well, on the gifting of the shares to anyone other than your spouse, you are deemed to receive proceeds of disposition equal to the fair market value of the shares.

If the value of the business has increased significantly over the years, a large capital gain will generally result. Such a gain is eligible for the lifetime capital gains exemption. There is an additional capital gains exemption of $400,000 over and above the normal $100,000 exemption. This additional exemption applies to gains realized on the disposition of "qualified farm property" or "qualified small business corporation shares". These are defined terms, but if your business is an active business carried on primarily in Canada, and more than 90 per cent of the fair market value of assets of the corporation are used in the business, chances are that it would qualify for the additional capital gain exemption. If your spouse owns part of the small business corporation, he or she also has a $500,000 exemption, which means that tax on up to $1,000,000 of capital gains may be eliminated. If the gain is realized in one particular year, however, you may effectively be subject to the alternative minimum tax (AMT) on the "untaxed" part of the gain.

Rollover of Farming Property

To encourage the children of farmers to continue to operate the family farm after their parents' retirement or death, special rules permit farming assets to be passed from one generation to the next without incurring a tax cost. Similar rollover rules also apply to the transfer of shares of a family farm corporation, or a holding corporation that owns such shares, and to an interest in a family farm partnership. Also, the additional $400,000 capital gain exemption is available for gains realized on the disposition of qualified farm property after 1984, to the extent it has not been used to shelter gains from the disposition of qualified small business corporation shares. You would opt to use the rollover provisions only if you expect to otherwise fully use your lifetime capital gains exemption. If not, transferring the property under the lifetime exemption will increase the child's tax cost of the property, resulting in a smaller capital gain whenever the child disposes of the property.

Estate Freezing Techniques

After deciding on the objectives that best suit your estate planning needs, particular techniques must be chosen that will achieve your intended objectives with the optimum tax advantage. The techniques briefly discussed below all involve "freezing" the present value of your business so that all or part of the future growth and the resulting tax consequences are deferred to your heirs. However, these techniques may be used to freeze the value of almost any assets having inherent taxable capital gains.

An estate freeze is generally undertaken when assets are likely to increase substantially in value over the long term. The goals of the freeze are usually to eliminate or defer, if possible, immediate tax in your hands, to ensure that future growth of the asset will benefit your children, and to allow you to maintain control of the asset. The lifetime capital gains exemption allows you to achieve the first goal either partially or wholly.

The choice of technique used to freeze the assets will depend upon a number of considerations, including:

- nature of the assets to be frozen;
- size of the estate;
- extent of control you wish to exercise over the frozen assets;
- number of parties to be involved in the freeze;
- immediate tax cost, if any, which might result from the freeze, bearing in mind access by you and your spouse to the lifetime capital gains exemption;
- degree of complexity that you can tolerate;
- professional fees that will be incurred;
- degree of flexibility and reversibility desired.

The following discussion assumes that your active business assets are owned by a corporation controlled by you. The corporate structure generally facilitates effective succession and estate planning. If business assets are not held by such a corporation, it is usually a relatively simple matter to arrange.

Direct Sale. Perhaps the simplest method of freezing your interest in shares of a privately held company is to sell the shares directly to your adult children. The sale would take place at fair market value, and you would take back a promissory note for the balance of the sale price not received in cash. There should be an agreement of purchase and sale that sets out the details of the sale, such as terms of payment, the due date of any unpaid amount, whether the unpaid balance is subject to interest, etc. It is not necessary to charge interest on the unpaid balance owed by your children, but the attribution rules will then apply.

One disadvantage of a direct sale is that you will be taxed on any capital gain realized in excess of any gain eligible for your lifetime capital gains exemption. You also may become subject to the alternative minimum tax. However, you may claim a reserve (i.e., exclude from income) on a portion of the taxable gain if you do not immediately receive all proceeds of disposition. When amounts claimed under the reserve provisions are eventually brought back into income for tax purposes, they will be eligible for your lifetime capital gains exemption, provided the shares were disposed of after 1984. Remember that even if you gift the shares to your children, you will be deemed to receive proceeds of disposition equal to their fair market value.

A second disadvantage of a direct sale is that you could lose control of the business, assuming sufficient voting shares are sold to your children. This may be overcome if you subscribe for new voting preferred shares that carry more votes than the existing common shares. Alternatively, you may be able to exercise some control by placing the common shares in escrow (i.e., maintaining possession and control of them) until the demand note has been entirely paid off.

Another disadvantage of a direct sale is that unless cash is paid for the shares, the amount owing to you remains with the corporation and may therefore continue to be at risk. A solution might be to have your children take out a loan to pay you for the shares, rather than accepting a demand note from them; however, this would necessitate recognizing the entire capital gain almost immediately for tax purposes and risks triggering the alternative minimum tax. As an alternative, the consideration could be part cash (from the outside loan) and part note (from the children).

Sale to a Holding Company. A common method of freezing the value of shares in an existing company involves the use of a new holding company specifically set up to acquire such shares. The children involved in the freeze would incorporate a company and acquire all its common shares for a nominal amount. You would transfer your shares in the operating company to the newly incorporated holding company, which generally can be done on a tax-deferred basis. You would take back voting preferred shares (with a value equal to the shares transferred into the holding company) in the new company as consideration for the transfer.

Over the last few years, changes in family law in certain provinces, in which assets acquired by a couple during their marriage are divided equally on dissolution of the marriage, could result in a significant portion of a parent's assets being transferred to the former spouse of a child. In order to circumvent this possibility, in the above scenario, the parent would acquire all the common shares of the holding company as well as the preferred shares. The parent would then gift the common shares to his or her child(ren). This would exclude the common shares from the matrimonial property of the married child in most instances, since assets inherited or received by way of gift are excluded from the matrimonial property. In Quebec, shares of a private or public company are not included in the matrimonial property.

Any future appreciation in the value from the operation of the business now accrues to your children. You could retain control of the operating company by means of voting preferred shares in the holding company. This permits you to set dividends and a reasonable salary according to your income requirements and allows you to run the business much as you did before.

One disadvantage of the use of a holding company in an estate freeze is that a capital gain or deemed dividend may arise on the redemption or disposition of the preferred shares (that you acquired as consideration for the transfer of your shares) during your lifetime. However, all or a portion of the capital gain may be exempt under your lifetime capital gains exemption. As well, it might be necessary to obtain a professional valuation of your shares.

Asset Freeze. As an alternative to transferring the shares of an operating company to a holding company, you may wish to consider freezing the value of these shares by selling the underlying operating assets to a new company incorporated by your children. This method of estate freezing may involve considerable work and expense, and sales or other transfer taxes could result. However, in some situations an asset freeze is the best approach. For example, you may own a multi-faceted business that you want to break up into separate corporations, each to be owned by one child.

Internal Freeze. It may be possible to reorganize the existing capital structure of your company to accomplish an estate freeze. Where the applicable provincial or federal companies law permits, you may exchange all your existing common shares for voting preferred shares of a certain type. Subsequent to this transaction, a new class of common shares is created that the children purchase at a nominal amount. The result of such a reorganization is that you freeze the current value of your holdings in the operating company, and your children participate in the future growth in value of the company through their ownership of the common shares. This type of freeze is relatively simple, does not require a new corporate entity, and provides you with preferred shares that should give you a fixed income, if desired. Of course, as with other freezes where no cash is received, there is always the problem that the money owed to you is tied up in the corporation and therefore exposed to some risk.

Choosing the Best Freeze Vehicle. Each of the methods of freezing an estate outlined above has its advantages and disadvantages. The final decision depends on your particular situation and should not be based solely on income tax considerations. For example, a partial estate freeze should provide better protection from future inflation than a complete freeze. In all cases, it is advisable for you to consult your professional advisors before making a final decision and proceeding with the necessary steps to put the plan into action. An estate freeze requires careful planning, not only because of the tax consequences involved, but because it may well be very difficult to thaw (i.e., unwind) the freeze once it has been effected.

Sales to Third Parties

If you own a business, you may want to transfer it to unrelated parties, such as fellow shareholders, partners, or key employees, rather than to your children or spouse. For one thing, your spouse or children may not be able or willing to run the business. The children may live a long distance away, have their own careers, or simply not be interested in taking over the business. Or the partners or other shareholders may not want the children involved.

Arranging a sale to employees may bind your best employees to the business, relieve you of some management headaches as you get older, and may assist in an orderly transfer of ownership. A sale could be coupled with a long-term employment contract should you wish to remain involved in the company.

Insurance and Buy-Sell Agreements

Insurance arrangements for business purposes are complex and require careful planning. The purpose of business insurance in the context of estate planning usually is to ensure that there are sufficient funds on hand at your death to enable the business to be dealt with in accordance with your wishes.

Depending on your estate plan, you may want to ensure that your estate will have sufficient liquid assets on hand to pay tax on any taxable capital gains realized on your death that are in excess of your available capital gains exemption. Furthermore, you may want your partner or another shareholder in the corporation to purchase your share of the business on your death.

Buy-Sell Agreement. A buy-sell agreement is basically a contract between business partners or shareholders of a corporation. It is frequently used in estate planning to ensure, for instance, that surviving shareholders have the right or obligation to purchase the shares of a deceased shareholder. It is advantageous both for the survivors, who may not want a stranger to buy into the corporation, and the family of the deceased, who might otherwise have difficulty selling the shares.

The spousal rollover rules are not applicable to shares that are subject to a compulsory buy-sell agreement, and tax would be paid by the deceased shareholder in the terminal tax return on any resulting capital gain if the lifetime capital gains exemption has been fully used. However, if the buy-sell agreement is structured in such a way that the surviving shareholder has an option to buy, and the surviving spouse has an option to sell, the shares can first pass to the spouse on a rollover basis. Any capital gain arising on the subsequent sale of the shares by the spouse would be recognized in his or her hands and be eligible for the spouse's own lifetime capital gains exemption.

Whichever buy-sell method is employed, one thing remains certain — unless there is some method of funding the transaction, the agreement may not be consummated. It is common for life insurance to be used as a means to provide the funds necessary to finance the sale. There are three common methods of employing life insurance as the funding mechanism for a buy-sell agreement.

Criss-Cross Insurance. This is an insurance arrangement where each shareholder of a corporation acquires a life insurance policy on the life of each other shareholder. On the death of one shareholder, the survivors receive the tax-free proceeds of the policy and use the funds to purchase the deceased's shares from his or her estate or beneficiaries. One disadvantage of this method is that the cost of the insurance to each shareholder can vary widely depending on the ages and health of the other shareholders.

Corporate-Owned Insurance. With this type of policy the corporation insures the lives of its shareholders and receives the proceeds on their deaths. The advantage of this method is that the corporation pays all the insurance premiums and the cost to the shareholders is shared in proportion to their shareholdings. The proceeds are used by the corporation to purchase the deceased's shares, either from the deceased's estate or from the surviving spouse. Generally, neither the deceased nor the spouse will be subject to tax on the buy-back if the arrangement is properly structured. However, the surviving shareholders do not have the cost base of their shares increased on the redemption, which in effect means the deceased's shareholder's gain has been transferred to them. This problem could be rectified by reducing the redemption price so that more cash is retained in the corporation or increasing the amount of the insurance.

Split-Dollar Insurance. Split-dollar insurance is a combination of both criss-cross and corporate-owned insurance. Each shareholder purchases a whole-life type of policy on the other and assigns the cash value of the policy to the company. On the death of a shareholder, the company receives the cash value of the policy while the surviving shareholders receive the face value less the cash value and use these proceeds to purchase the shares. The advantage of this method is that the company pays most of the premiums.

The use of buy-sell agreements, combined with life insurance funding, should be an integral part of any estate plan where shares of private companies are owned and there are two or more shareholders dealing with each other at arm's length and also in some non-arm's length situations. In all cases, the insuring method employed should not be chosen without the assistance of a professional advisor.

Beginning the Process. Estate planning is not a once-and-for-all activity. You should view it as an ongoing process, involving a variety of techniques over the years, to suit your changing circumstances. This chapter has focused on the tax aspects of estate planning. There are other factors for you to consider that are of equal or greater importance. Above all, don't rush into a tax-motivated estate plan without giving full consideration to your personal and financial circumstances. Keep in mind that few things in life turn out exactly as we plan them. Your estate plan must have sufficient flexibility built into it so that you can adapt it to fit unforeseen future events.

11. Special Tax Measures for Quebec Residents

In general, the Quebec government harmonizes its tax legislation with that of the federal government. On the other hand, there are some differences, especially as regards personal income tax credits. Details of these credit amounts and a few other features particular to the Quebec system are outlined in Chapter 12.

Unlike the federal legislation, which grants tax credits for some items, Quebec legislation provides for the deduction of these items in computing net or taxable income.

Finally, the Quebec government has tax benefits available to its residents that are offered concurrently by the federal government or are uniquely adapted to the economic needs of the province. They are designed to promote investments in strategic sectors of industry such as mining exploration, film production, scientific research, business capitalization, etc.

This chapter discusses certain specific tax measures that apply to Quebec residents.

Deductions, Tax Credits, Refunds, and Reductions

Employment Income. Quebec legislation provides for the deduction of unemployment insurance premiums paid and for contributions to the Quebec Pension Plan in computing net employment income, whereas federal legislation allows an individual tax credit. Quebec legislation also provides another employment deduction that is not found in federal legislation: a 6 per cent expense deduction is allowed on income, to a maximum of $750.

Some annual dues are also deductible only under Quebec legislation. Of note are annual dues to an association of employees recognized by the Minister whose main objective is the study, safeguarding and promotion of the economic interests of its members and also payments required for membership in an artistic association recognized by the Minister.

Finally, when employment duties are performed outside Canada in certain types of businesses (construction, engineering, etc.), federal legislation allows a tax credit while Quebec legislation provides for a deduction. In both cases, certain conditions must be met in order to have access to these tax benefits.

Tuition Fees. Tuition fees are also treated differently in Quebec. When fees exceed $100, a tax credit equal to 17 per cent is allowed under the federal system. Where the credit is not fully claimed, it may be transferred to a spouse or parent to a maximum of $600.

Under Quebec legislation, tuition fees must be deducted when computing net income and can be claimed only by the student. Moreover, starting in 1990, examination fees charged by professional corporations mentioned in Schedule 1 of the Professional Code, i.e., exclusive professions and professions with reserved titles, are deductible when the examinations are required to become a member of one of the corporations or to practise one of the professions mentioned in the Schedule.

Charitable Gifts. Charitable gifts present another example of varying tax treatment. Under federal legislation, the first $250 of a donation is credited at 29 per cent. Quebec legislation provides a deduction used in computing taxation income.

Other Items. Some items contained in the Quebec legislation do not have a federal equivalent.

To compensate for a portion of the fuel tax, holders of valid taxi permits are eligible for a special tax credit of $500 per permit.

A person who resides in Quebec on December 31 may be entitled to a real estate tax refund. This credit is available to tenants and homeowners. The size of the credit depends on the individual's total income and that of the spouse, if applicable. It also depends on the aggregate of real estate taxes for the year. For 1990, the maximum credit has been set at $460 ($660 for couples 60 years of age and over who receive the Guaranteed Income Supplement or Spouse's Allowance).

Finally, low and middle income families are entitled to a tax reduction. This provides a reduction of income tax, but is not refundable. The amount of the reduction depends on the individual's total income, that of the spouse, and that of any dependent children (if applicable). For 1990, the maximum has been set at $710 per person or $1,180 for a couple with at least one dependent child. Single parents who do not share an independent dwelling with another adult are entitled to a tax reduction of $925.

Quebec Stock Savings Plan

In 1979 the Quebec government introduced the stock savings plan (QSSP) to promote stock investments in Quebec companies and reduce the tax burden on individuals residing in the province. The QSSP is an agreement concluded with a broker in securities or other authorized person who is entrusted with the custody of the qualifying shares according to the client's instructions. Although the QSSP has undergone several adjustments over the years that have made it much less attractive, it nevertheless remains an interesting method of tax planning if you are prepared to acquire shares on the stock market. It is wise to keep in mind, however, that any tax benefit achieved may decline with the market value of the shares. Consequently, even when shares qualify under the QSSP, the first criterion prior to purchasing shares is still to consider their potential yield and growth. To reduce the risk associated with this type of investment, you can invest through a stock savings plan investment group or investment fund. One of the advantages of these alternative forms of investment is that you will have a share in a more diversified stock portfolio without having to make a considerable investment.

Tax Benefit. If you are a Quebec resident at the close of the tax year and have acquired qualifying shares in a stock savings plan during the year, you may deduct the adjusted cost of these shares from your taxable income, to a maximum of 10 per cent of your total income. Your "total income" is the net income amount that appears on your provincial income tax return, less the capital gains exemption used during the year. Shares must have been acquired prior to the end of the tax year and be included in the stock savings plan before February 1 of the following year to be considered as qualifying shares. The allowable deduction is restricted to the adjusted cost of your shares: that is, to the percentage of the cost of the shares (excluding the cost of borrowing, brokers' commissions, or safekeeping fees), which is determined according to the class of shares issued and the size of the issuing corporation. The more uncertain the financial position of the corporation, the greater the share rights conferred upon their holders and the higher the percentages. The following list shows the maximum percentage applicable to each class of corporation.

Regional venture capital corporation	125%
Developing corporation (Assets of between \$2 million and \$50 million or shareholders' equity of between \$750,000 and \$20 million)	100%
Large corporation (Assets above \$250 million)	50%
Other corporations	75%

The percentages may be less when the shares these corporations issue carry fewer rights.

For example, you purchase shares in a stock savings plan for \$4,000, of which only 75 per cent of the purchase cost is an eligible deduction. This year your net income is \$50,000, and you realized a taxable capital gain of \$10,000 for which the capital gains exemption has been used. Your QSSP deduction will amount to the lesser of the following:

- Adjusted cost of shares $4,000 × 75% $ 3,000
- 10% of your total income
  10% × ($50,000 - $10,000) $ 4,000

Your deduction will therefore be $3,000.

To encourage people to invest in shares of small and medium-size businesses in particular, the total amount that can be deducted with respect to the acquisitions of shares in major corporations or restricted shares has been set at $1,000 annually. Thus, if over the year you acquire shares in major corporations amounting to $3,000, which allows you a 50 per cent deduction, you can use only a $1,000 deduction instead of the $1,500 deduction. The excess $500 cannot be deferred to another year.

Management fees for a QSSP and the cost of borrowing to purchase shares constitute financial expenses and are deductible annually.

Additional Deductions. Shares included in a QSSP entitle the holder to an additional 25 per cent deduction on the cost of the shares when they are acquired under an employee stock option plan. An employer may create a plan to encourage employees to acquire the shares issued by the employer corporation when it goes public. The plan must be available to all employees and executives with more than three months of service and who own less than 5 per cent of the capital stock of the corporation immediately prior to acquiring shares in the stock option plan.

An additional deduction is given for shares included in a QSSP when the proceeds of sale are used to finance research and development activities (R&D) in Quebec of the issuing corporation. This particular deduction will be discussed later in this chapter.

Recovery of Deductions. You must keep shares in your stock portfolio that have an adjusted cost equal to the amount for which you obtained a deduction for at least two full calendar years (this does not include the additional deduction for R&D). Should you fail to do so, you will either have to include a portion or all of the deductions previously allowed in your income for the year in which this condition is not met, or reduce the amount of the deduction that you could otherwise claim during the year.

If, for example, during the year you acquire $1,000 of shares that are deductible at 50 per cent and you sell these shares the following year, you must, before the following year ends, acquire replacement shares with an adjusted cost of $500 so that the deduction you obtained will not be added to your income during the current year. Therefore, you can acquire shares for $500 that are fully deductible. You cannot, however, benefit from a new QSSP deduction for the replacement shares.

Previously, only newly issued shares could be used as replacement shares. Since June 1, 1988, shares of developing corporations that already entitled the holder to the QSSP deduction may also be used for this purpose if they are purchased on the secondary market and listed by La Commission des valeurs mobilières du Québec.

Capital Gains and Dividends. Dividends received on shares in stock savings plans are treated as any other dividend received on shares. When the shares are sold, the capital gain or loss is calculated in the usual manner. The tax benefit received does not reduce the actual cost of the shares.

QSSPs versus RRSPs. Unlike the RRSP, which allows for income tax payments to be deferred, the advantage of the QSSP is that it offers a real tax saving so long as the conditions enumerated above are met. The RRSP does, however, reduce your immediate income tax at both the federal and provincial levels, while the QSSP deduction can be used only in Quebec.

A share in a QSSP cannot be included under another tax plan at the same time. However, you can contribute successively to your QSSP and RRSP using the same funds, and because the deadlines for contributions are different, obtain the QSSP and the RRSP deduction for the same year.

While shares included in a QSSP must be acquired before year end, it is possible to contribute to an RRSP right up until the end of February of the subsequent year. As a result, QSSP shares can be sold at the beginning of the year following the year of acquisition and the sale proceeds used to make a contribution to an RRSP. To avoid the recovery of deductions, QSSP shares must be replaced before the end of the year in which they are sold, unless the adjusted cost of shares for over two years in your QSSP portfolio allows you to escape this rule. The double deduction is therefore only temporary, but may prove useful if you do not have sufficient liquid assets available at this time of the year.

Cooperative Investment Plan

To encourage investments in certain Quebec cooperatives, the provincial government has introduced the Quebec Cooperative Investment Plan, which provides a deduction to an individual who acquires eligible securities issued by a qualified cooperative. This deduction applies only to a member or worker of the cooperative.

The deduction and the two-year holding period are calculated in the same manner as under the QSSP. The deduction is equal to 100 per cent of the cost of the securities purchased, not exceeding 10 per cent of total income.

When a cooperative sets up a "stock ownership plan" (i.e., a plan allowing employees and officers to acquire securities in their cooperative) similar to the one discussed above in the section "Quebec Stock Savings Plan", individuals who acquire such securities are entitled to an additional deduction of 25 per cent, for a total deduction of 125 per cent of the cost of the shares.

Quebec Business Investment Companies

In 1985, another investment vehicle, the QBIC (Quebec Business Investment Companies) was launched to offset the weak capitalization of provincial private corporations. A QBIC is a business incorporated in Quebec whose primary activity is to acquire shares of other unrelated eligible private corporations operating mainly in a specific sector such as manufacturing, tourism or export in Quebec. QBICs are an intermediate financing vehicle between eligible private corporations and investors. QBICs are not listed on the stock market.

Tax Benefit. If you are a Quebec resident on December 31 of a tax year and purchase common shares of a QBIC, you will be entitled to deduct 100 per cent of your purchase price from your taxable income for Quebec income tax purposes, provided it corresponds to your financial commitment.

However, this deduction can be taken only when the QBIC invests the money to acquire common shares of an eligible corporation. An additional 25 per cent deduction may be allowed in accordance with the investments the QBIC will make in small or medium-size businesses located outside of main urban centres. Moreover, if the QBIC shares are acquired as part of an employee stock option plan under which employees are encouraged to purchase shares of the employer corporation through a QBIC, another 25 per cent deduction will be granted. Thus the total deduction could reach 150 per cent.

However, the deduction used in a given year must not exceed 30 per cent of your total income; any portion not claimed in a year due to this limit may be deferred to the five subsequent years.

As with the QSSP, there is an additional deduction allowable under the QBIC when the money invested is used to finance research and development activities. This deduction will be discussed in more detail later in this chapter.

Investments in a QBIC do not affect contribution limits to RRSPs and QSSPs. Unlike a QSSP, you are not required to keep your securities for at least two years. This is the responsibility of the QBIC. If a QBIC constitutes an "active business" and the other criteria prescribed by law are met, you can even benefit from the additional $400,000 capital gains exemption on the sale or disposal of these shares.

In spite of these tax benefits, investing in this type of tax shelter is still not widespread for several reasons, among them the absence of a secondary market for QBIC shares once the deductions are used.

Savings and Credit Union Permanent Shares Savings Plan

In order to assist savings and credit unions to finance their growth, a savings and credit union permanent shares savings plan was introduced in 1989 and is scheduled to be in effect for three years. Under the plan, you are entitled to deduct from your taxable income, solely for Quebec purposes, 100 per cent of the cost of newly issued permanent shares, to a maximum of $1,000 in 1989 and $2,000 in 1990 and 1991 for a total deduction of $5,000 during the life of the plan. The deduction is granted to the first purchaser of the security during the taxation year or within 60 days after the end of the taxation year. Shares must be held for a minimum of two years, and the deduction will not be included in calculating cumulative net investment losses.

Research and Development (R&D)

For both federal and provincial income tax purposes, you can benefit personally from R&D tax benefits only if you operate your own business. However, there are interesting tax benefits, other than the regular deductions, for acquiring QSSP or QBIC securities that are available when the proceeds of the share issuance are used to finance a corporation's research and development activities in Quebec.

To promote R&D financing through issuing capital stock using outside venture capital, the Quebec Government grants additional deductions to private investors who acquire these shares. These deductions may represent up to 50 per cent or 100 per cent of qualified R&D expenditures (according to both the size of the corporation that stands to benefit from this financing and the type of R&D) on the condition that the R&D expenditures were made and the corporation waives its own tax credit for these expenditures. It is, in fact, a mechanism that allows for transferring the tax credits of the corporation to investors. These additional deductions in no way modify a QSSP or QBIC, nor do they affect the adjusted cost of the shares that must be included in the QSSP portfolio. These deductions are also not subject to the annual applicable limits for a QBIC or QSSP; however, the additional deduction must be limited to an amount so that the total deduction granted with respect to a security does not exceed 200 per cent. Furthermore, these additional deductions receive favourable treatment, since they may be deferred to subsequent years.

R&D Venture Capital Corporation

In addition to QSSP and QBIC shares, the Quebec Government has created a special vehicle to finance R&D. These

R&D Venture Capital Corporations are corporations that must raise funds almost exclusively to finance the R&D projects of small and medium-size businesses in Quebec.

Anyone who buys shares of this type of corporation is entitled to a 100 per cent basic deduction on the cost of the shares when the R&D expenditure is made, plus an additional 50 per cent or 100 per cent R&D deduction, as applicable, if the corporation incurring the expenditure waives its tax credit. The basic deduction may not exceed 30 per cent of one's total income, but the unused portion may be deferred to a future year. There is no limit to the additional deduction, which can also be deferred to subsequent years.

Unlike the QSSP, there is no minimum holding period in order to be able to take full advantage of the deductions.

Certified Quebec Films

The Quebec Government allows you to claim 30 per cent of your investment in a Canadian film production annually as capital cost allowance. However, to support the Quebec film industry in particular, the rate can reach a maximum of 166 2/3 per cent when the investment is used to produce a certified Quebec film. This deduction may be used as soon as the first year of acquisition. The requisite conditions to obtaining certification for the film are notably that the producer, main actors and creative personnel reside in Quebec.

The deduction is computed according to the risk assumed by the investor:

Guaranteed Portion of Investment	Allowable Deduction
less than 45%	166 2/3%
45% to 55%	133 1/3%
55% to 70%	100%
more than 70%	30%

When these investments are acquired as shares in a limited partnership, a capital gain is often realized at the time of their disposal. This gain is usually more important for calculating Quebec income given the tax benefits that are offered.

Mineral Exploration and Oil and Gas Sectors

The acquisition of flow-through shares, whether directly or through a limited partnership, enables the holder to benefit from tax breaks for Quebec income tax purposes. Additional deductions are also allowed for exploration expenses incurred in Quebec before the end of 1991, subject to a 60-day grace period. Thus, surface mining exploration expenses incurred in Quebec up to the end of 1991 may allow for a deduction equal to 166 2/3 per cent of these expenses.

Strategic Economic Investments Account

As discussed in the introduction to this chapter, many of the tax benefits found in the Quebec legislation are designed to promote investments in strategic sectors of the Quebec economy.

To encourage individuals to take advantage of these tax benefits, the various deductions used throughout the year are regrouped in a special account called the "strategic economic investments account". These deductions include:

- Quebec stock savings plan (QSSP);
- cooperative investment plan (CIP);
- Quebec business investment companies (QBIC);
- saving and credit union permanent shares savings plan;
- additional deduction in respect of R&D;
- additional deduction for R&D/QSSP;
- additional deduction for R&D/QBIC;
- R&D venture capital corporations;
- certified Quebec films (CCA and additional deductions), and
- additional deduction in respect of Quebec resources.

The regrouping of items under the strategic economic investments account has two advantages. Firstly, the total of these items is not taken into account when computing the cumulative net investment losses for the Quebec income tax return (the concept of "cumulative net investment losses" is discussed in Chapter 7). Consequently, the deductions in the strategic economic investments account do not reduce the amount of capital gains exemptions otherwise available in the individual's Quebec income tax return.

Secondly, under the rules for the alternative maximum tax, in addition to the basic $40,000 minimum tax exemption, an individual who makes investments described in that account can deduct a further exemption of up to 15 per cent of his or her total income. For this purpose, total income means net income less capital gains deduction used in the year in computing income.

Family Patrimony

As of July 1, 1989, married persons are required to take into consideration the new rules recently adopted under Bill 146 with respect to economic equality between spouses in the event there is a partition of family patrimony, whether through separation from bed and board, dissolution or annulment of a marriage, or death.

These rules generally affect the partition of certain property between the spouses, not on the basis of individual property but on the net value of the property, by creating a right of claim between the spouses.

The property that is part of the partition is the family's principal and secondary residences, household furniture, motor vehicles used for family travel, and the benefits accrued during the marriage under public or private retirement plans. Any of the above-mentioned property that has been acquired before or during the marriage by way of succession, legacy, or gift is excluded from the family patrimony.

In the case of tax and estate planning, a spouse who makes a bequest to the other spouse should consider the implications of the partition of family patrimony. In addition to the bequest, the spouse will be entitled to 50 per cent of the net value of the property which is part of the family patrimony.

Corporations Operating in Quebec

Tax Rates. In Chapter 8, we discussed the tax as well as the planning advantages that are available through the incorporation of a business. It was mentioned that the tax structure varies depending on the province in which the income was earned as well as on the type and amount of income.

Under Quebec legislation, the basic corporate rate is 13 per cent. However, active business income is subject to a tax reduction, the "small business deduction" (SBD). For such deduction, the Quebec Taxation Act makes reference to the definitions contained in the federal legislation rather than repeating them. Thus, where a corporation claims the SBD in its federal tax return, a 10 per cent reduction is provided under the Quebec Taxation Act. However, where active business income is not subject to the federal SBD, a reduction of 7.5 per cent is provided.

However, a surtax is payable in addition to the rates mentioned above, which raises the effective corporate income tax rate. For 1990, the surtax was 12 per cent until April 26 and increased to 15 per cent after that date.

The following schedule summarizes the effective corporate income tax rates:

	Active Business Income					
	Eligible for SBD		Not eligible for SBD		Other Income	
Basic rate	13.00%	13.00%	13.00%	13.00%	13.00%	13.00%
Deduction allowed	10.00	10.00	7.50	7.50	–	–
Rate before surtax	3.00	3.00	5.50	5.50	13.00	13.00
12% surtax from 1/1/90 to 4/26/90	0.36	–	0.66	–	1.56	–
15% surtax after 4/26/90	–	0.45	–	0.83	–	1.95
Effective rate	3.36%	3.45%	6.16%	6.33%	14.56%	14.95%
Average effective tax rate for 12/31/90 year end	3.42%		6.28%		14.83%	

Exemptions for New Corporations. To stimulate the formation of new firms in Quebec, provincial legislation provides an income tax exemption to certain corporations. This tax exemption applies to the first three taxation years of new corporations with respect to active business income otherwise subject to the low rate of 3.45 per cent mentioned before.

A corporation qualifies for the exemption in a taxation year if:

- it was incorporated after May 1, 1986;
- it is not the result of an amalgamation;
- the year is one of its first three taxation years;
- a tax return is filed within six months after the end of its first taxation year.

However, a corporation is not eligible to the exemption for the year if, among other things, it:

- was associated with any other corporation;
- was not a "Canadian-controlled private corporation";
- carried on a personal services business;
- carried on an eligible business as a member of a partnership.

Research and Development. To encourage research and development (R&D) in Quebec, provincial legislation provides several refundable tax credits to all corporations who carry out R&D in the province.

The basic credit is 20 per cent of wages paid in Quebec for R&D activities in Quebec. If a corporation meets certain criteria and if the expenses are incurred pursuant to particular activities, the rate is increased to 40 per cent for corporations whose assets are less than $25 million or whose net shareholders' equity does not exceed $10 million, and to 40 per cent of all R&D expenses incurred in Quebec pursuant to:

- a university research contract;
- a pre-competitive research project;
- a catalyst project recognized by the Government and certified by the Technological Development Fund, with the possibility of obtaining rents equal to 50 per cent of other eligible expenditures;
- an environmental technology innovation project that has received Technological Development Fund certification (with the possibility of grants equal to 40, 50 or 100 per cent of other eligible expenditures).

Training. To encourage corporations to provide training for their personnel, Quebec legislation provides several refundable tax credits to all corporations for eligible training expenses incurred. An enhanced credit is available for certain small and medium-size companies that do not have assets in excess of $25 million or a shareholders' equity in excess of $10 million.

In general, eligible training expenses include the cost of a human resources development plan (HRDP), costs incurred with an eligible training establishment, and wages paid to an employee when the training activity takes place during regular working hours, including travelling costs.

For small and medium-size businesses, the rate of the refundable tax credit is 30 per cent of the cost of the HRDP and 20 per cent for other training costs and wages. Large businesses receive 20 and 10 per cent respectively for the same expenses. For the years 1990, 1991 and 1992, these rates will be increased by 20 per cent for eligible training expenses incurred during these years by small and medium-size businesses and 10 per cent for expenses incurred by large businesses during the same period.

In general, eligible training expenses are those incurred after April 26, 1990. In the case of the cost of an HRDP, only contracts entered into after August 31, 1990, are eligible.

12. Facts and Figures for Calculating 1990 Taxes

PROVINCIAL RATES OF TAX FOR 1990 (1)

British Columbia	51.5%	Nova Scotia	59.5* (4)
Alberta	46.5* (2)	Prince Edward Island	57.0* (6)
Saskatchewan	50.0* (7)	Newfoundland	62.0
Manitoba	52.0* (3)	Yukon	45.0
Ontario	53.0* (5)	Northwest Territories	44.0
New Brunswick	60.0	Non-Residents	52.0

* Surtaxes and Flat Tax not included (8)

Notes

1. Rates are expressed as a percentage of basic federal tax. The rates are those in effect at the date of publication. At that time Manitoba was the only province that had not yet tabled a provincial budget. A subsequent budget may contain amendments which change tax rates and other items which affect provincial tax.
2. Alberta levies a 0.5% flat tax on taxable income and an 8% surtax (not applicable on flat tax) on Alberta tax in excess of $3,500.
3. In Manitoba, a 2% flat tax is calculated on net income. As well, a 2% surtax is calculated on net income in excess of $30,000 (i.e. there is a basic credit of $600 - additional credits may apply).
4. Nova Scotia imposes a 10% surtax on provincial tax in excess of $10,000.
5. A 10% surtax applies to Ontario tax in excess of $10,000.
6. Prince Edward Island imposes a 10% surtax on provincial tax in excess of $12,500.
7. Saskatchewan levies a 2% flat rate tax on net income. A 12% provincial surtax applies to Saskatchewan tax in excess of $4,000.
8. There are tax reductions for lower levels of income in several of the provinces, including Alberta, Manitoba, Ontario and Saskatchewan.

FEDERAL RATES OF TAX FOR 1990**

Taxable Income	Tax	On Next
$0	0 + 17%	$28,275
28,275	4,807 + 26	28,275
56,550	12,158 + 29	Excess

**Table does not incorporate the federal surtax of 5% on all federal tax and the additional 3% surtax on federal tax in excess of $15,000. Beginning in 1991, the additional surtax will increase to 5% and will apply to federal tax in excess of $12,500.

QUEBEC PERSONAL INCOME TAX MEASURES

1990 FEDERAL TAX – QUEBEC ONLY

Taxable Income	Tax	On Next
$0	$0 + 15.05%	$28,275
28,275	4,255 + 23.01	28,275
56,550	10,760 + 25.67	9,800
66,350	13,275 + 26.54	Excess

The tables takes into account the federal surtax and the 16.5% Quebec tax abatement.

1990 QUEBEC PROVINCIAL TAX

Taxable Income	Tax	On Next
$0.00	$0 + 16.0%	$7,000
7,000	1,120 + 19.0	7,000
14,000	2,450 + 21.0	9,000
23,000	4,340 + 23.0	27,000
50,000	10,550 + 24.0	Excess

QUEBEC TAX VALUE OF 1990 PERSONAL TAX CREDITS

Basic	$1,056	
Person living alone	188	(1)
Married	1,056	(2)
Person 65 or over	440	
Dependent children		
General		
1st child	466	(2) (3)
2nd child and subsequent children	403	(2) (3)
Post-secondary studies	295	(4)
Single parent family	233	(2) (3) (5)
Other dependants		
General	403	(2) (6)
Disabled	1,056	(2) (7)
Mental or physical impairment	440	
Member of a religious order	792	

Notes:
1. Credit available for an individual who is not entitled to the married credit and who maintains a self-contained domestic establishment in which no person other than the individual or a person eligible for the dependent children credit lived during the year.
2. The net income of the dependant reduces the tax credit.
3. Children under 18 or studying full-time.
4. Credit for each term, maximum of two terms.
5. Credit available for an unmarried individual or, if married, does not support or live with his or her spouse and is not supported by his or her spouse. Moreover, the individual does not live maritally with any person and maintains a self-contained domestic establishment where he or she lives and supports a person eligible for the dependent children credit. This credit can be added to the credit for dependent children.
6. Any person 18 or over who is connected with the taxpayer by blood relationship, marriage or adoption.
7. This credit cannot be added to the general tax credit for other dependants.

OTHER QUEBEC CREDITS AND DEDUCTIONS

Employment deduction: the lesser of 6 per cent of employment income and $750.

Pension tax credit: the lesser of 20 per cent of eligible pension income and $200.

Quebec pension plan and unemployment insurance contributions are deductible in computing net income since they were not converted into tax credits. The same is true for charitable donations: the deduction is maintained for donations not exceeding 20 per cent of net income.

The deduction for tuition fees is also maintained for Quebec tax purposes. Moreover, tuition fees may not be transferred to another person for Quebec tax purposes.

The Quebec tax credit for medical expenses is 20 per cent (17 per cent for federal tax purposes).

QUEBEC ALLOWANCES FOR NEWBORN AND ADOPTED CHILDREN

1st child	$ 500
2nd child	1,000 (1)
3rd child and subsequent children	6,000 (2)

Notes
1. This allowance is payable in two instalments of $500. The first instalment is payable when the child is born and the second on the child's first birthday.
2. The allowance is payable in sixteen quarterly instalments of $375 each.

1990 COMBINED FEDERAL AND PROVINCIAL PERSONAL TAX RATES (5)

TAXABLE INCOME		Alberta (1,2,3) Prov. rate 46.5%		British Columbia Prov. rate 51.5%		Manitoba (1,2,3) Prov. rate 52.0%		New Brunswick Prov. rate 60.0%		Newfoundland Prov. rate 62.0%		Nova Scotia Prov. rate 59.5%		Northwest Territories Rate 44.0%	
From (A)	To (B)	Tax on (A)	Rate on Excess (B-A)	Tax on (A)	Rate on Excess (B-A)	Tax on (A)	Rate on Excess (B-A)	Tax on (A)	Rate on Excess (B-A)	Tax on (A)	Rate on Excess (B-A)	Tax on (A)	Rate on Excess (B-A)	Tax on (A)	Rate on Excess (B-A)
$ 0	$ 6,170	$ 0	0.00%	$ 0	0.00%	$ 0	0.00%	$ 0	0.00%	$ 0	0.00%	$ 0	0.00%	$ 0	0.00%
6,171	6,600	0	17.85	0	26.61	0	17.85	0	28.05	0	28.39	0	27.97	0	25.33
6,601	6,900	77		114		77		120		122		120		109	
6,901	7,000	130		194		130		205		207		204		185	
7,001	7,598	148		221		148		233		235		232		210	
7,599	8,025	255		380		255	30.69	401		406		400		362	
8,026	8,951	332		495		387		521		528		520		471	
8,952	9,213	497		740		671		780		790		778		705	
9,214	10,000	544	30.46	811		752		855		865		852		772	
10,001	14,000	783		1,019		992		1,074		1,087		1,071		970	
14,001	16,036	2,001		2,083		2,220		2,196		2,223		2,189		1,983	
16,037	21,500	2,622	26.26	2,626		2,846		2,769		2,802		2,760		2,500	
21,501	23,000	4,056		4,078		4,521	28.69	4,300		4,352		4,287		3,883	
23,001	28,275	4,449		4,477		4,952		4,721		4,778		4,706		4,263	
28,276	30,000	5,836	39.89	5,883	40.69	6,467	42.82	6,202	42.90	6,278	43.42	6,184	42.77	5,601	38.74
30,001	38,646	6,524		6,584		7,205	44.82	6,942		7,026		6,921		6,268	
38,647	42,772	9,973		10,102		11,080		10,651		10,780		10,618		9,618	
42,773	50,000	11,619	40.86	11,781		12,930		12,421		12,572		12,384		11,217	
50,001	56,550	14,572		14,722		16,169		15,522		15,710		15,475		14,016	
56,551	69,968	17,248	45.51	17,387	45.39	19,105	49.53	18,332	47.85	18,554	48.43	18,276	47.71	16,554	43.21
69,969	76,197	23,354	46.38	23,477	46.26	25,750	50.40	24,752	48.72	25,052	49.30	24,677	48.58	22,352	44.08
76,198	83,306	26,243		26,357		28,889		27,786		28,122		27,702	50.30	25,097	
83,307	93,864	29,541		29,646		32,473		31,250		31,627		31,156		28,231	
93,865 and over		34,439		34,530		37,794		36,394		36,833		36,284		32,885	

TAXABLE INCOME		Ontario (1,2) Prov. rate 53.0%		Prince Edward Island (1) Prov. rate 57.0%		Quebec (4) See page 207		Saskatchewan (1,2,3) Prov. rate 50.0%		Yukon Rate 45.0%		Non-Residents Rate 52.0%	
From (A)	To (B)	Tax on (A)	Rate on Excess (B-A)	Tax on (A)	Rate on Excess (B-A)	Tax on (A)	Rate on Excess (B-A)	Tax on (A)	Rate on Excess (B-A)	Tax on (A)	Rate on Excess (B-A)	Tax on (A)	Rate on Excess (B-A)
$ 0	$ 6,170	$ 0	0.00%	$ 0	0.00%	$ 0	0.00%	$ 0	0.00%	$ 0	0.00%	$ 0	0.00%
6,171	6,600	0	17.85	0	27.54	0	15.04	0	17.85	0	25.50	0	26.69
6,601	6,900	77		118		65	31.04	77		110		115	
6,901	7,000	130		201		158		130	28.35	186		195	
7,001	7,598	148		228		189	34.04	159		212		221	
7,599	8,025	255		394		393		329		365		382	
8,026	8,951	333	44.88	512		539		450		474		496	
8,952	9,213	747	26.86	766		853		712		710		743	
9,214	10,000	818		839		943		787		777		813	
10,001	14,000	1,029		1,055		1,210		1,009	33.35	977		1,022	
14,001	16,036	2,103		2,156		2,572	36.04	2,343	28.35	1,997		2,090	
16,037	21,500	2,651		2,718		3,307		2,922		2,517		2,634	
21,501	23,000	4,117		4,222		5,276		4,469		3,909		4,091	
23,001	28,275	4,520		4,635		5,816	38.04	4,895		4,292		4,492	
28,276	30,000	5,939	41.08	6,090	42.12	7,824	46.01	6,392	42.30	5,639	39.00	5,902	40.82
30,001	38,646	6,647		6,815		8,617		7,121		6,311		6,605	
38,647	42,772	10,199		10,457		12,595		10,778	44.10	9,683		10,134	
42,773	50,000	11,894		12,195		14,494		12,598		11,292		11,819	
50,001	56,550	14,863		15,239		17,819	47.01	15,785		14,111		14,769	
56,551	69,968	17,554	45.82	17,998	46.98	20,899	49.67	18,674	48.93	16,665	43.50	17,443	45.53
69,969	76,197	23,702	46.69	24,302	47.85	27,562	50.54	25,239	49.80	22,502	44.37	23,552	46.40
76,198	83,306	26,609		27,282		30,710		28,340		25,265		26,441	
83,307	93,864	29,929	48.23	30,684		34,303		31,881		28,420		29,740	
93,865	and over	35,021		35,736	49.50	39,638		37,139		33,104		34,640	

Notes

1. A surtax applies on provincial tax as follows:
   Alberta — 8% on Alberta tax (excluding flat tax) in excess of $3,500;
   Manitoba — 2% flat rate on net income in excess of $30,000;
   Ontario — 10% on Ontario tax in excess of $10,000;
   Prince Edward Island — 10% on PEI tax in excess of $12,500;
   Saskatchewan — 12% on Saskatchewan tax in excess of $4,000.
2. A low income tax reduction applies. Reductions are phased out as income increases, which in certain cases results in an increased marginal tax rate. We have taken into account only the portion of the reduction that applies to all taxpayers.
   - We have taken into account only the basic $200 Saskatchewan sales tax reduction (other reductions are based on family situation and age). The Saskatchewan reduction is zero at zero taxable income and rises to a maximum of $200 at taxable income of $6,900 to $10,000, then from there, drops back to zero at taxable income of $14,001.
   - The Alberta reduction is zero at zero taxable income and rises to a maximum of $287 at taxable income of $9,213, then from there, drops back to zero at taxable income of $16,036.
   - The Manitoba reduction is zero at zero taxable income and rises to a maximum of $287 at taxable income of $7,598, then from there, drops back to zero at taxable income of $21,500.
   - The Ontario reduction is zero at taxable income of $6,171 (no Ontario tax before then, since no flat tax) and rises to a maximum of $167 at taxable income of $8,025, then from there, drops back to zero at taxable income of $8,951.
3. A flat tax of 0.5% is applied to taxable income in Alberta. In Manitoba and Saskatchewan, a flat tax of 2% applies to net income. In the latter two cases, we have assumed that net income is equal to taxable income.
4. For purposes of comparison, we have assumed that taxable income for federal and Quebec purposes is the same. Taxpayers resident in Quebec receive a 16.5% abatement of federal tax.
5. Federal surtax is included in these rates and, in determining the brackets at which the rates apply, we have applied the personal federal tax credit of $1,049.

MARGINAL TAX RATES FOR CAPITAL GAINS (1) 1990

Taxable Income	B.C.	Alta.	Sask.	Man.	Ont.	Que.
$28,276 - $30,000	30.52%	29.92%	31.73%	32.12%	30.81%	34.51%
30,001 - 37,700	30.52	29.92	31.73	33.62	30.81	34.51
37,701 - 38,646	30.52	29.92	31.73	33.62	30.81	34.51
38,647 - 42,772	30.52	29.92	33.08	33.62	30.81	34.51
42,773 - 50,000	30.52	30.64	33.08	33.62	30.81	34.51
50,001 - 56,550	30.52	30.64	33.08	33.62	30.81	35.26
56,551 - 69,967	34.04	34.14	36.70	37.15	34.37	37.25
69,968 - 75,400	34.69	34.79	37.35	37.80	35.02	37.90
75,401 - 76,197	34.69	34.79	37.35	37.80	35.02	37.90
76,198 - 83,306	34.69	34.79	37.35	37.80	35.02	37.90
83,307 - 93,290	34.69	34.79	37.35	37.80	36.17	37.90
93,291 - 93,863	34.69	34.79	37.35	37.80	36.17	37.90
93,864 - Excess	34.69	34.79	37.35	37.80	36.17	37.90

Taxable Income	N.S.	N.B.	P.E.I.	Nfld.	Yukon	N.W.T.	Non-Res.
$28,276 - $56,550	32.08%	32.18%	31.59%	32.57%	29.25%	29.06%	30.62%
56,551 - 69,967	35.78	35.89	35.23	36.32	32.63	32.41	34.15
69,968 - 76,197	36.43	36.54	35.89	36.98	33.28	33.06	34.80
76,198 - 93,863	37.73	36.54	35.89	36.98	33.28	33.06	34.80
93,864 - Excess	37.73	36.54	37.13	36.98	33.28	33.06	34.80

1. Rates include federal tax, federal surtax, provincial taxes (including surtaxes and flat taxes) and Quebec 16.5% abatement.

MARGINAL TAX RATES FOR DIVIDENDS (1) 1990

Taxable Income	B.C.	Alta.	Sask.	Man.	Ont.	Que.
$28,276 - $30,000	24.78%	24.61%	27.04%	27.36%	25.02%	31.68%
30,001 - 37,700	24.78	24.61	27.04	29.86	25.02	31.68
37,701 - 38,646	24.78	24.61	27.04	29.86	25.02	31.68
38,647 - 42,772	24.78	24.61	28.29	29.86	25.02	31.68
42,773 - 50,000	24.78	25.20	28.29	29.86	25.02	31.68
50,001 - 56,550	24.78	25.20	28.29	29.86	25.02	32.93
56,551 - 69,967	30.65	31.02	34.33	35.75	30.94	36.25
69,968 - 75,400	31.24	31.61	34.92	36.33	31.53	36.84
75,401 - 76,197	31.24	31.61	34.92	36.33	31.53	36.84
76,198 - 83,306	31.24	31.61	34.92	36.33	31.53	36.84
83,307 - 93,290	31.24	31.61	34.92	36.33	32.57	36.84
93,291 - 93,863	31.24	31.61	34.92	36.33	32.57	36.84
93,865 Excess	31.24	31.61	34.92	36.33	32.57	36.84

Taxable Income	N.S.	N.B.	P.E.I.	Nfld.	Yukon	N.W.T.
$28,276 - $56,550	26.05%	26.13%	25.65%	26.44%	23.75%	23.59%
56,551 - 69,967	32.21	32.31	31.73	32.70	29.38	29.18
69,968 - 76,197	32.80	32.90	32.31	33.29	29.96	29.77
76,198 - 93,863	33.97	32.90	32.31	33.29	29.96	29.77
93,864 - Excess	33.97	32.90	33.43	33.29	29.96	29.77

1. Rates include federal tax, federal surtax, provincial taxes (including surtaxes and flat taxes), federal and provincial dividend tax credits and Quebec 16.5 per cent abatement. For federal tax purposes, the dividend tax credit is equal to 13-1/3 per cent of the grossed-up amount of taxable dividends. For Quebec tax purposes, the credit is equal to 8.87 per cent of this same amount.

Personal Tax Credits for 1990 - Combined Federal and Provincial Tax Value (1)

	Federal credit	B.C.	Alta.	Sask.	Man.	Ont.	Que.	N.S.	N.B.	P.E.I.	Nfld.	Yukon	N.W.T.	Non-Res.
		51.5%	46.5%	50.0%	52.0%	53.0%	(10)	59.5%	60.0%	57.0%	62.0%	45.0%	44.0%	52.0%
Basic	$1,049	$1,642	$1,589	$1,626	$1,647	$1,657	$1,984	$1,726	$1,731	$1,699	$1,752	$1,574	$1,563	$1,647
Person living alone							188							
Married (2)	874	1,368	1,324	1,355	1,372	1,381	1,830	1,438	1,442	1,416	1,460	1,311	1,302	1,372
Persons 65 or over	566	886	857	877	889	894	941	931	934	917	945	849	843	889
Married equivalent (2)	874	1,368	1,324	1,355	1,372	1,381	774	1,438	1,442	1,416	1,460	1,311	1,302	1,372
Dependent children under 19 (9)														
General														
1st and 2nd child (3)	68	106	103	105	107	107	526	112	112	110	114	102	101	107
3rd and additional children (4)	136	213	206	211	214	215	524	224	224	220	227	204	203	214
Post-secondary studies (11)							295							
Single parent family							233							
Other dependants														
Age 18 or over on first day of year							403							
Disabled over 18 (5)	257	402	389	398	403	406	1,284	423	424	416	429	386	383	403
Disability	566	886	857	877	889	894	941	931	934	917	945	849	843	889
Education / per month (6)	10	16	15	16	16	16	9	16	17	16	17	15	15	16
Pension income (7)	170	266	258	264	267	269	351	280	281	275	284	255	253	267

Tuition Fees (%) (12)	17	26.61	25.76	26.35	26.69	26.86	N/A	27.97	28.05	27.54	28.39	25.50	25.33	26.69
Medical expenses (%) (8)	17	26.61	25.76	26.35	26.69	26.86	35.05	27.97	28.05	27.54	28.39	25.50	25.33	26.69
Charitable donations (12) up to $250 (%)	17	26.61	25.76	26.35	26.69	26.86	N/A	27.97	28.05	27.54	28.39	25.50	25.33	26.69
excess (%)	29	45.39	43.94	44.95	45.53	45.82	N/A	47.71	47.85	46.98	48.43	43.50	43.21	45.53
CPP contributions (12)	17	26.61	25.76	26.35	26.69	26.86	N/A	27.97	28.05	27.54	28.39	25.50	25.33	26.69
UIC contributions (12)	17	26.61	25.76	26.35	26.69	26.86	N/A	27.97	28.05	27.54	28.39	25.50	25.33	26.69

Notes

1. Combined amounts based on provincial tax rate as shown and federal surtax of 5%, provincial surtaxes ignored.
2. Reduced where spouse's or qualifying dependant's net income is between $514 and $5,655 and eliminated if income exceeds $5,655. In Quebec, the tax credit is reduced by the net income of the dependant.
3. Reduced if child's income is between $2,570 and $2,969 and eliminated if child's income exceeds $2,969. In Quebec, $463 for the second child, and the tax credit is reduced by the net income of the dependant.
4. Reduced if child's income is between $2,570 and $3,368 and eliminated if child's income exceeds $3,368. In Quebec, the tax credit is reduced by the net income of the dependant.
5. At end of year. Credit is not in addition to other credit for dependants.
6. Credit for each month of full-time attendance at a post-secondary school or university.
7. Reduced where qualifying pension income is less than $1,000 (credit is 17% of qualified pension income to a maximum of $170; 20% in Quebec, maximum $200).
8. 17% (20% in Quebec) of medical expenses in excess of lesser of $1,543 and 3% of net income.
9. At end of year. In Quebec, include children studying full-time.
10. Credits calculated taking into account 16.5% federal abatement.
11. Credit for each term (maximum 2 terms).
12. For Quebec tax purposes, the deduction is maintained instead of being converted into a tax credit.

1990 INDIVIDUAL TAX CALCULATION

Calculation of Total Income		
Income from Employment	$50,000	
Income from Other Sources		
Family Allowance payments	816	
Interest income	1,000	
Total Income		$51,816
Calculation of Taxable Income		
Deductions from Total Income		
Registered pension plan contributions	$ 2,000	
Registered retirement savings plan premiums	1,500	
Total Deductions		3,500
Taxable Income		$48,316
Summary of Taxes and Credits		
Federal Tax		$10,018
Federal Tax Credits		
UI/CPP contribution credits	$ 204	
Charitable contribution credits	115	
Basic credit	1,049	
Spousal credit	874	
Dependants credit	136	
Total Tax Credits		2,378
Basic Federal Tax		$ 7,640
Federal Surtax		382
Total Federal Tax Payable		$ 8,022
Ontario Tax Payable		4,049
Total Taxes Payable		$12,071

Assumptions

1. Taxpayer is married.
2. Spouse has no income.
3. Taxpayer supports two children under 18, who have no income.
4. Charitable contributions are $500.
5. Canada Pension Plan and Unemployment contributions total $1,200.

INDEX

Offices in Canada

Deloitte & Touche Offices

Brampton	(416) 455-7616
Calgary, Scotia Centre	(403) 267-1700
Calgary, Kensington	(403) 267-1800
Charlottetown	(902) 566-2566
Cornwall	(613) 932-5421
Dartmouth	(902) 468-2000
Edmonton	(403) 421-3611
Fredericton	(506) 458-8105
Guelph, Practice Office	(519) 824-1190
Guelph, Insolvency Office	(519) 824-5010
Guelph, Consulting Office	(519) 822-1090
Halifax	(902) 422-8541
Hamilton	(416) 523-6770
Hawkesbury	(613) 632-4178
Kitchener	(519) 576-0880 (519) 579-2520
Langley	(604) 534-7477
London	(519) 679-1880
Markham	(416) 475-4100
Mississauga	(416) 275-4000 (416) 275-3224
Moncton	(506) 857-8400
New Westminster	(604) 664-6200
North York	(416) 229-2100
Oshawa	(416) 579-8202
Ottawa	(613) 236-2442 (613) 563-0321
Ottawa East	(613) 746-9703
Pickering	(416) 831-1244
Prince Albert	(306) 763-7411
Prince George	(604) 564-1111
Regina	(306) 525-8791
Saint John	(506) 632-1080
Sarnia	(519) 336-6133
Saskatoon	(306) 652-7071 (306) 244-8900
Scarborough	(416) 293-7704
St. Catharines	(416) 688-1841
St. John's	(709) 576-8480
St. Thomas	(519) 631-8250
Sydney	(902) 564-4517
Toronto	(416) 364-4242 (416) 861-9700
Vancouver	(604) 669-3343 (604) 669-4466
Victoria	(604) 386-2164
Waterloo	(519) 747-3207
Windsor	(519) 258-8833
Winnipeg	(204) 942-0051
Woodbridge	(416) 851-3946

Samson Bélair/Deloitte & Touche Offices

Alma	(418) 668-8325
Amos	(819) 732-8273
Baie-Comeau	(418) 589-5761
Chibougamau	(418) 748-2684
Chicoutimi	(418) 549-6650
Dolbeau	(418) 276-0133
Drummondville	(819) 477-8945
Farnham	(514) 293-5327
Gatineau	(819) 243-6020
Granby	(514) 372-3347
Grand-Mère	(819) 538-1721
Hull	(819) 770-3221
Jonquière	(418) 542-9523
La Malbaie	(418) 665-3965
Lac-Etchemin	(418) 625-5921
Laval	(514) 333-8840 (514) 668-8910
Longueuil	(514) 670-4270
Matagami	(819) 739-2589
Matane	(418) 566-2637
Montreal	(514) 393-7115
Québec	(418) 624-3333 (418) 681-7231
Rimouski	(418) 724-4136
Roberval	(418) 275-2111
Rouyn-Noranda	(819) 762-0958
Saint-Hyacinthe	(514) 774-4000
Senneterre	(819) 737-2614
Sept-Îles	(418) 968-1311
Shawinigan	(819) 537-7281
Sherbrooke	(819) 564-0384
St-Félicien	(418) 679-4711
Trois-Pistoles	(418) 851-2232
Trois-Rivières	(819) 691-1212
Val d'Or	(819) 825-4462
Ville de La Baie	(418) 544-7313
Ville St-Georges	(418) 228-6676

National Offices

Toronto (King Street West)	(416) 599-5399
Toronto (Wellington Street)	(416) 861-9700
Montreal	(514) 393-7115